I BELONG

I BELONG
Volume 2

Biblical Reflections on Statelessness

Edited by Semegnish Asfaw

I Belong, Volume 2
Biblical Reflections on Statelessness
Edited by Semegnish Asfaw

WCC Publications is the book publishing programme of the World Council of Churches. The WCC is a worldwide fellowship of 352 member churches which represents more than half a billion Chris-tians around the world. The WCC calls its member churches to seek unity, a common public witness and service to others in a world where hope and solidarity are the seeds for justice and peace. The WCC works with people of all faiths seeking reconciliation with the goal of justice, peace, and a more equitable world.

Opinions expressed in WCC Publications are those of the authors.

Scripture quotations are from the New Revised Standard Version Bible, © copyright 1989 by the Division of Christian Education of the National Council of the Churches of Christ in the USA. Used by permission.

Production: Lyn van Rooyen, coordinator WCC Publications
Cover design: Based on a design by Julie Kauffman Design
Cover Art: The Storm

> John August Swanson
> Giclee, 19.75" x 29"
> JohnAugustSwanson.com

Based on design by Michelle Cook / 4 Seasons Book Design; typesetting by Beth Oberholtzer
ISBN: 978-2-8254-1780-5

World Council of Churches
150 route de Ferney, P.O. Box 2100
1211 Geneva 2, Switzerland
www.oikoumene.org

Printed and bound by CPI Group (UK) Ltd, Croydon, CR0 4YY

CONTENTS

PREFACE

As we journey through the World Council of Churches' Pilgrimage of Justice and Peace, we are constantly reminded that our Christian faith calls us to be inclusive and to look after those on the margins. The destitute. The overlooked.

Millions of stateless people around the world live on the margins of the margins because they are not recognized as citizens by any country. This lack of legal identity, which translates into a lack of identification documents, puts them in a state of increased vulnerability: statelessness means that these individuals and communities do not legally exist. As a result, they do not have access to all the basic rights that we take for granted, such as having a birth certificate, getting married, buying property, travelling, enjoying civic and political rights, or even something as simple as owning a cell phone – for which an identification card is often required.

Discrimination and exclusion are at the root of statelessness. In most cases, statelessness results from discrimination against ethnic, religious, or linguistic minorities who are singled out by a state that does not want to recognize them as its citizens. Statelessness can also result from gender inequality in nationality laws which do not give equal rights to men and women when it comes to conferring nationality upon their children or spouse.

Discrimination and exclusion are negative forms of power and domination that aim at singling out vulnerable individuals or communities. It is about coercion, control, arbitrariness. When a state decides to render stateless a community living on its territory, it is not only a form of rejection but is also a domination technique through which the state demonstrates its power in order to preserve hierarchies by silencing others. When a community is rendered legally invisible, its members are unseen, forgotten, excluded, ostracized.

The publication of biblical reflections on belongingness helped us navigate various aspects of statelessness though the lens of biblical scriptures. This second publication of biblical reflections on statelessness presents new perspectives that did not appear in the first volume. Indigenous voices and the meaning of land is one contribution in particular that we invite you to explore.

I am grateful to the authors for enriching this publication with their contributions. Some of these texts were biblical reflections done during regional workshops we organized in different parts of the world. Others were the product of a direct invitation to the author to challenge them to reflect on an issue somewhat new to them and therefore to help us formulate a new understanding of the vulnerability that statelessness represents.

The art work on the cover, The Storm, reflects the reality of many stateless people. It also portrays the words of Pope Francis in his 2021 message for the World Day of Migrants and Refugees:

> *"We are all in the same boat and called to work together so that there will be no more walls that separate us, no longer others, but only a single 'we', encompassing all of humanity."*[1]

We hope that readers will find in these texts useful tools for discussion and reflection during Bible studies in congregations and communities around the world.

Semegnish Asfaw
October 2021

---

1. "Pope calls for joint efforts on path towards an ever wider "we," Vatican News, Accessed 23 December 2021, https://www.vaticannews.va/en/pope/news/2021-05/pope-francis-migrants-refugees-wider-we-world-day-message.html.

CONTRIBUTORS

Dr Stylianos D. Charalambidis teaches Ecumenical Movement at the School of Social Theology and Christian Culture of Aristotle University of Thessaloniki. He holds a BA in Theology, a BA in Law, and a PhD in Theology.

Juan C. Chavez-Quispe is an Aymara theologian and anthropologist serving as a member of the Ecumenical Indigenous Peoples' Reference Group. He is an alumnus of the Ecumenical Institute at Bossey and published papers and book chapters on Indigenous Peoples' history, cultural heritage, and spiritualities, as well as on Andean Theology. He has taught at Universidd Mayor de San Andrés and ISEAT Institute.

The Rev. Fr Dr Lawrence Iwuamadi (Nigerian) is a Roman Catholic priest who has been seconded by the Pontifical Council for Promoting Christian Unity, Vatican, to the Ecumenical Institute at Bossey and the World Council of Churches, Geneva, Switzerland since 2012. A New Testament scholar, Fr Lawrence teaches Ecumenical Biblical Hermeneutics and Intercultural Biblical Studies at Bossey. He is a member of the *International Dialogue between the Catholic Church and Classical Pentecostal* and serves as the Catholic member of the board of *Fondation du Forum Chrétien Mondial*.

The Rev. Kelli Deniqua Jolly Is an itinerant presbyter, ordained to the ministry of Word and sacrament. She is a pastoral caregiver and advocate for human rights - holding fast to a belief in the love of God for all creation and a need for the church to play an active role in freeing all of God's people from all forms of oppression. She believes that these are the foundation of a meaningful existence along with the charge of the prophet Micah from God to God's people in Micah 6:8 ". . . and what does the Lord require of you but to do justice, and to love kindness, and to walk humbly with your God?"

Dr Elizabeth Joy is a member of the Malankara Orthodox Syrian Church. She is the former executive secretary for Mission Education, Council for World Mission. She is currently a director and trustee at the Churches Together in England and a member of the Council of Reference at British SCM.

Thandi Soko-de Jong is a Malawian theologian living in the Netherlands. Her work focuses on bringing her experiences as a female, African theologian into conversation with intercultural theology.

The Rev. Dr Konrad Raiser is a former general secretary of the WCC and retired professor of ecumenical theology. He is the authors of numerous books and articles including "*Religion, Power, Politics*" and "*The Challenge of Transformation.*"

Maina Talia is a lay person and a climate activist from Vaitupu, Tuvalu. He is currently completing his doctoral studies at Charles Sturt University in Australia. His research interests are on *Muna o te fale* (Indigenous Knowledge), *tuakoi* (neighbour), geopolitics, and climate change.

The Rev. Dr. Karen Georgia A. Thompson is an elected officer in the United Church of Christ, serving as the Associate General Minister (AGM) for Wider Church Ministries (WCM) and co-executive for Global Ministries. She is an inspiring preacher and theologian, who shares her skills and gifts in a variety of settings nationally and internationally, often using her poetry as a part of her ministry. She earned her Doctor of Ministry degree from Seattle University.

CHAPTER 1

NO LONGER STRANGERS AND ALIENS BUT CITIZENS AND MEMBERS OF GOD'S HOUSEHOLD

KONRAD RAISER

At its 10th Assembly in Busan in 2013, the World Council of Churches (WCC) adopted the "Statement on the Human Rights of Stateless People."[1] The opening paragraph refers to article 15 of the Universal Declaration of Human Rights[2] as "a foundation of identity, human dignity, and security. Nationality is an essential prerequisite to the enjoyment and protection of the full range of human rights."[3]

In article 15, the Declaration states: "Everyone has the right to a nationality." It may be surprising that in formulating the document, the writers considered it necessary to state as a "right" what under normal circumstances would be regarded as self-evident. The large majority of people obtain their nationality at birth from their parents. They consider it a given which they

---

1. World Council of Churches, "Statement on the Human Rights of Stateless People" (2013), https://www.oikoumene.org/sites/default/files/Document/PIC%2002_2%20 ADOPTED%20Human%20Rights%20of%20Stateless%20People.pdf.

2. United Nations, "Universal Declaration of Human Rights" (1948), https://www.un.org/ en/about-us/universal-declaration-of-human-rights.

3. Erlinda N. Senturias and Theodore A. Gill, Jr, eds, *Encountering the God of Life: Report of the 10th Assembly of the World Council of Churches* (Geneva: WCC Publications, 2014), 273, https://www.oikoumene.org/resources/documents/report-of-the-wcc-10th-assembly.

do not call into question. Rather, it is accepted as the basis for developing a national identity that expresses the positive feeling of belonging to a larger community: to a country with its people, its language and history, its traditions and customs. It thus becomes the "foundation of identity."

The Declaration, however, adds a second sentence: "No one shall be arbitrarily deprived of his nationality nor denied the right to change his nationality." This addition points to the fact that what seems to be self-evident for most people constitutes a vital problem for human persons and groups who are regarded as stateless – a large and growing number of people. They have either been deprived of a nationality by decision of the country in which they reside, or their parents have not been able, due to political and legal restrictions, to transmit their nationality to their offspring. In many countries, a woman who is married to a stateless man is not allowed to transmit their nationality to their children, who thus become stateless. Wherever they live, they are regarded as aliens and denied a sense of belonging and of the protection that is implied in the recognition of nationality.

The right to a nationality reflects the modern condition where the nation-state has become the dominant form of political organization of large communities. This is a relatively recent development in human history that became generalized as a consequence of the French Revolution. The nation-state took the place of earlier forms of organization of human groups in clans or tribes, in chiefdoms or principalities, in kingdoms or empires. People were subjects of the respective rulers and had no independent rights. Their sense of belonging and identity were linked to the land they owned or on which they worked and to the kinship ties of extended families or tribes. The original understanding of the term "nation" still reflects this link to a particular ethnic origin, as in the distinction of different groups in the medieval universities. The former large empires also included different nations with their distinct languages and territories in one comprehensive political framework.

A special case in this development of political organization involved the city republics which emerged in the 13th-century in Italy and then spread through medieval Europe. They brought back to life the tradition which was established in the Greek city states and continued in Rome. Here the full sense of belonging took the form of citizenship. It was reserved for owners of property and implied the right of participation in decision making about the life and order of the city. In the French Revolution, this notion of citizenship was adopted for all free "citizens" who were no longer subject to the power of the king. Since then, citizenship is distinguished from nationality in countries where the right to participation in political decision making depends on meeting particular conditions. In most countries with a democratic constitution, nationality and citizenship are considered identical.

The progressive establishment of nation-states implied the definition of borders around a given state territory. In the post-colonial nation-states in Africa, Asia, and Latin America, the borders – which in many instances had been defined by the colonial powers – separated ethnic groups with their inherited identity and imposed a "nationality" on people whose sense of belonging was linked to their traditional community. In many of the new nation-states, efforts to create a national identity led to treating such "minority groups" as aliens in the respective country and depriving them of their right to a nationality. The WCC statement on the human rights of stateless people refers to the case of the Rohingya, who have been arbitrarily made stateless by the government of Myanmar and are caught between Myanmar and Bangladesh. There are also large ethnic communities that have not been able to establish a recognized state and now find themselves divided between several newly created nation-states, such as the Kurds, who are divided among Turkey, Syria, Iraq, and Iran. Another case are the Roma people, who still live in large families or clans and have never formed a larger political and administrative structure. They have traditionally travelled among several countries, especially in Central and South-eastern Europe, and are subject to discrimination as stateless people. Finally, there are migrant workers in countries like Nepal, Côte d'Ivoire, and the Dominican Republic who, after being residents in their respective countries for more than a generation, were arbitrarily deprived of nationality and treated as stateless.

The WCC statement characterizes statelessness in the following terms:

> Stateless people live in a situation of legal limbo. Without protection from any state, stateless people are often exploited and – particularly women and children – may be more vulnerable to smuggling, harassment, and violence. Since they are not recognized and registered as citizens of any country, stateless people are also denied concomitant rights such as the right to reside legally, to register the birth of a child, to receive education and medical care and to access formal employment and housing. Stateless people are also often not allowed to own property, to open a bank account, or to get married legally. Stateless people face constant travel restrictions as well as social exclusion. Due to the lack of citizenship in any country, our stateless sisters and brothers face numerous daily hardships – needless separation from their families, and fundamental uncertainty about what their lives might hold or the ability to pursue their hopes and ambitions.
>
> As a result, not only are stateless persons denied their rights and faced with living in limbo, but their situation is rarely recognized by mainstream society. The feeling of being invisible leads to a debilitating sense of desperation. As a result of their plight, many stateless persons are forced to cross international borders and become refugees.[4]

The statement recognizes that the situation of statelessness and disputed nationality can ultimately be resolved only by governments. In determining issues of citizenship, governments must, however, observe and conform to general principles of international law, such as the United Nations' Convention on the Reduction of Statelessness,[5] which has been ratified by 73 states. With the Convention Relating to the Status of Stateless Persons,[6] it establishes basic principles and standards for the protection of stateless people.

---

4. World Council of Churches, "Statement on the Human Rights of Stateless People," 3–4.

5. United Nations, Convention on the Reduction of Statelessness (1961), https://www.un.org/en/genocideprevention/documents/atrocity-crimes/Doc.25_reduction%20statelessness.pdf.

6. United Nations, Convention Relating to the Status of Stateless Persons (1954), https://www.unhcr.org/ibelong/wp-content/uploads/1954-Convention-relating-to-the-Status-of-Stateless-Persons_ENG.pdf.

In considering statelessness as a violation of fundamental human rights, the WCC statement appeals to the churches to raise awareness of the situation of stateless people and to advocate for the protection of their human rights. It also points out that the churches, through the biblical tradition and their own history, share a particular sensitivity to the situation of the alien which goes beyond their general commitment to human rights. Reference is being made to the central position in the Torah of Israel: "You shall not wrong or oppress a resident alien, for you were aliens in the land of Egypt" (Ex. 22:21). The critical role of the relationship to the stranger appears also in Jesus' parable of the last judgement: "I was a stranger and you welcomed me" (Matt. 25:35).

However, it is not only the biblical tradition which urges upon the churches a particular solidarity with stateless people as strangers and aliens in their midst. There is also the recollection of the situation of the early Christian community, who in the first centuries were discriminated against, persecuted, and treated as aliens in their communities. They considered themselves "aliens and exiles" among the gentiles (1. Pet. 2:11); their true citizenship or commonwealth was in heaven (Phil. 3:20). Like the patriarchs of ancient Israel, they saw themselves as resident aliens (Heb. 11:9). This self-identification as part of the "wandering people of God" is reflected even in the later designation of a local Christian community as a "parish." The word has its root in the Greek term *paroikia*, which refers to the living space of a resident alien in a foreign setting. It is this identity to which the letter to the Ephesians refers, in the words that were chosen as a title for these reflections. It proclaims that through the peace and reconciliation brought by Christ, the dividing wall between Christians and Jews has been abolished, and therefore the followers of Christ are "no longer strangers and aliens, but . . . [co-]citizens with the saints and also members of the household of God" (Eph. 2:19).

These brief references to the biblical witness serve as an invitation to deepen the reflection about Christian identity in its relationship to the experience of being a stranger, an alien, or even stateless. In modern times, statelessness is the most dramatic expression of the elementary experience of lacking a recognized identity, of not belonging to a community of mutual support and security. This experience is being shared by a growing number of refugees and migrants, many of whom are threatened with becoming stateless as well. An earlier WCC statement referred to these groups as "uprooted people."[7]

Statelessness in its modern form is a condition not known in biblical times. Citizenship as an equivalent to nationality was considered an important value, as demonstrated by apostle Paul when, in the court hearings before the Roman governors Felix and Festus, he appealed to the imperial court in Rome, arguing that he was a Roman citizen (Acts 22:26-29). However, the biblical record of the Hebrew people takes us back to the time before the emergence of nation-states or the large city republics of Athens and Rome. The Bible traces the origin of the later people of Israel to Abram (later Abraham) who was called by God to leave his country, his kindred, and his father's house and to move to a land that God was to show him (Gen. 12:1-9). The experience of coming as a stranger and alien to a foreign land continued, as Abraham was obliged to move further down to Egypt due to a famine in the land where he had intended to settle. The same experience of being on the move and living as aliens or even in exile is reflected in the stories of Isaac and Jacob and their descendants. The remembrance of the exile in Egypt and of God having liberated the people from the hand of Pharaoh became the foundation for the identity of the people of Israel.

Contemporary biblical scholarship helps us to read and understand these foundational stories not so much as a record of history in the modern sense, but rather as a narrative of collective memories about the origin and existence of the people of Israel caught in the constant power struggles between large neighbouring empires. From initial large families and migrant clans, they began to form kingships like their neighbouring communities. But these structures were constantly threatened in their existence by the expansive power struggles between the empires of Assur, Babylonia, and Egypt. Having to deal

---

7. Cf. statement by WCC central committee in 1995, in: http://www.wcc-coe.org/wcc/what/international/uprooted/moment1.html

with refugees and successive experiences of exile or diaspora were the marks of the precarious existence of the people. Their sense of identity and of belonging to the land of promise drew its strength from their faith and the recognition of the power of their God. Because God, out of love, had chosen the people while they were weak and threatened in their existence as aliens, they accepted it as a calling and commandment from God that the strangers and aliens in their midst had to be treated with particular care and given their full rights.

The Hebrew term for the stranger or alien (*gēr*) refers to people who live in a place where they do not originally belong, where they have no kindred or property and therefore are without rights and without legitimate access to the structures of dispute settlement. The term is used without ethnic or national connotations; it can refer to members of the people of Israel who have become refugees after the end of the northern kingdom or to people who belong to a different ethnic group or religion and were forced to migrate because of famine or wars.

The explicit rules for relating to the stranger and alien occupy a central place in all three collections of commandments in the Torah (Ex. 22:20, 23:9; Deut. 10:17-19; Lev. 19:33-34). In all instances, reference is made to the experience of having been strangers themselves in Egypt; therefore Israel "know[s] the heart of an alien" (Ex. 23:9). The basic commandment to love one's neighbour as oneself (Lev. 19:18) is even extended to the alien: "The alien who resides with you shall be to you as the citizen among you: you shall love the alien as yourself, for you were aliens in the land of Egypt; I am the Lord your God" (Lev. 19:34). Because God "loves the strangers, providing them with food and clothing" (Deut. 10:18), Israel should extend the same love to the stranger and alien. This implies that the resident alien should enjoy the same rights as the Israelites: "you and the alien shall be alike before the Lord. You and the alien who resides with you shall have the same law and the same ordinance" (Num. 15:15-16). Thus, even while they do not own property and do not belong to a family, they should enjoy the same rights and protection as if they were members of the people.

The book of Ruth includes a beautiful story about treating a stranger according to the same rules as the people of the land. Ruth was a young woman from the land of Moab. Her mother-in-law, Naomi, had moved to Moab with her husband and their two sons because of a famine in Judah. After Naomi's husband, Elimelech, died, the two sons took Moabite wives. Ten years later, both of the sons died as well. When Naomi decided to return to her homeland, she urged her daughters-in-law to remain in Moab. Ruth, out of love and loyalty to her mother-in-law, responded: "Where you go, I will go; where you lodge, I will lodge; your people shall be my people, and your God my God" (Ruth 1:16). After they arrived in Judah, Naomi advised Ruth to go and glean in the fields behind the reapers of Boaz, a relative on her husband's side. Boaz, after having learned who the young women was, instructed his servants not to bother her but to give her full hospitality. Being surprised at this treatment, Ruth said to Boaz: "Why have I found favour in your sight, that you should take notice of me, when I am a foreigner?" (2:10). Boaz, in recognition of her loyalty to her mother-in-law, which had moved her to leave her native land and to come to a people she did not know before, replied: "May the Lord reward you for your deeds, and may you have a full reward from the Lord, the God of Israel, under whose wings you have come for refuge!" (2:12). The story continues with Boaz acquiring a piece of land that had belonged to Elimelech, Ruth's deceased father-in-law. To maintain the dead man's name on his inheritance, he also took Ruth as his wife. While she was still a foreigner, she was assured of belonging to the people.

The way of relating to and receiving the stranger and alien thus occupies a central position in the Torah of Israel. It is of critical significance for the people's relationship with God. Because God loves the stranger with the same love as God loves the people, the stranger and alien can even be regarded as a bearer of God's presence. This is reflected in the ancient story of Abraham receiving and showing hospitality to the three men in whom he recognizes the presence of God (Gen. 18). The story continues with two of the men or angels moving on to Sodom; there they were granted hospitality by Lot, who was himself a resident alien in the city (Gen. 19). When people from the city threatened to use violence against Lot and his guests, the two men responded with the power of God: "the Lord has sent us to destroy [the city]" (Gen. 19:13). To disregard the commandment to show hospitality to the stranger means rejecting God and drawing God's wrath. This is remembered in the letter to the Hebrews when it says: "Let mutual love continue. Do not neglect to show hospitality to strangers, for by doing that some have entertained angels without knowing it" (Heb. 13:1-2).

Providing hospitality to the stranger or simply to visitors who were passing through became an accepted rule in the early Christian community, continuing established Jewish practice. The apostle Paul, when describing the conduct of the Christian community in his letter to the Romans, gives particular attention to hospitality: "Contribute to the needs of the saints; extend hospitality to strangers" (Rom. 12:13). The same advice appears in the first letter of Peter: "Be hospitable to one another without complaining" (1 Pet. 4:9). The Acts of the Apostles, referring to the travels of Paul and Peter, frequently mention the hospitality they received when arriving as strangers in a new place.

However, this openness to the stranger, in particular those not observing the ordinances of the Torah, became a point of contention between the Jewish majority and the emerging Christian community – and within the Christian community. The early Christians sought to follow in the way of Jesus. The gospels report how Jesus disregarded the limits of contact with strangers or those living at the margins of the Jewish community. He invited himself into the house of the tax collector Zacchaeus (Luke 19:5) and sought the company of those regarded as sinners according to the Torah. He allowed a Canaanite woman from the region of Tyre and Sidon to convince him of the need to heal her daughter (Matt. 15:21-28), and he responded willingly to the appeal of the Roman officer in Capernaum to heal his son (John 4:46-54). Jesus did not refuse contact with the Samaritan woman; he spoke with her about the proper way of worshipping God (John 4:1-42) and, seeing the presence of God's love and faith among people beyond his own, he revealed himself as the saviour of the world.

Through his challenge to the exclusive and restrictive interpretation of the Torah and to the claims of identity based on descent from Abraham (John 8:37-59), he became himself a stranger and outcast in his hometown and among his own people (Matt. 13:54-58; Luke 4:22-24; Matt. 8:20). The parable of the last judgement places him among the poor, the outcast, and the strangers: "I was thirsty and you gave me something to drink, I was a stranger and you welcomed me" (Matt. 25:35). The Gospel of John even opens its account by presenting Jesus as the incarnate word of God: "He came to what was his own, and his own people did not accept him" (John 1:11). The Gospel of Matthew, in recounting the birth and childhood of Jesus, sees him exposed to persecution by King Herod and forced into exile in Egypt (Matt. 2:13-15), while Luke, in his gospel, places Jesus' birth in a stable or outbuilding because there was no place in the inn to receive him and his parents (Luke 2:7).

The Acts of the Apostles describe the process by which the early Christian community began, following the example of Jesus, to reach out to people beyond their Jewish community of origin. The encounter of Peter with the Roman centurion Cornelius in Joppa, guided by a vision about eating unclean animals, raised the question about the lawfulness of contact with uncircumcised Gentiles (Acts 10). While the message of Peter about God, accepting people in all nations who fear him and do what is right, and proclaiming Jesus Christ was approved by the Holy Spirit, who fell upon those present (10:44-48), the question of reaching out to those beyond the Jewish community later became a potentially divisive issue between the apostles Peter and Paul and with the community in Jerusalem. The issue was resolved at the Council of Jerusalem, which gave conditional approval to Paul's mission among those who were regarded as strangers (Acts 15). As a result of the progressive separation between the emerging Christian and the original Jewish communities that enjoyed the status of a recognized community in the Roman empire, the Christian communities themselves became "strangers" and suffered the same rejection as their master. As mentioned earlier, they considered themselves "aliens and exiles" among the gentiles (1 Pet. 2:11). Their identity was based not on owning property, not on kinship or belonging to an ethnic group, but on identification with Jesus Christ as the incarnation of God's love. It was an identity that transcended "national" or cultural and ethnic lines of distinction. Their true citizenship or commonwealth was in heaven (Phil. 3:20).

Against this background, the Christian communities of the first three centuries provided a new sense of belonging to those who were living as strangers or outcasts in the larger community and refused to observe the ritual of emperor worship as the official symbol of collective identity. They endured persecution and accepted the existence in diaspora. When Constantine and his successors in the fourth century began to recognize the Christian community and their faith as the common religion of the Roman empire, this had profound consequences for the Christian sense of identity and how to relate to those outside the community. The earlier practice of hospitality and of welcoming strangers was continued in the emerging monastic communities, while the churches as institutional bodies with close links to the respective political structures progressively lost the sense of a transnational identity that transcended the boundaries of state and nation. It is one of the significant fruits of the modern ecumenical movement that the churches have begun to confront all forms of racism, ethno-centrism, and exclusive nationalism and to accept again their biblical call to welcome the stranger and to present themselves as inclusive communities.

CHAPTER 2

STATELESSNESS AND *UBUNTU*: IN DIALOGUE WITH PHILIPPIANS 2:1-4

THANDI SOKO-DE JONG

If then there is any encouragement in Christ, any consolation from love, any sharing in the Spirit, any compassion and sympathy, make my joy complete: be of the same mind, having the same love, being in full accord and of one mind. Do nothing from selfish ambition or conceit, but in humility regard others as better than yourselves. Let each of you look not to your own interests, but to the interests of others. (Phil. 2:1-4)

Ubuntu [the essence of being human] speaks particularly about the fact that you can't exist as a human being in isolation. It speaks about our interconnectedness. You can't be human all by yourself, and when you have this quality – Ubuntu – you are known for your generosity. We think of ourselves far too frequently as just individuals, separated from one another, whereas you are connected and what you do affects the whole world. When you do well, it spreads out; it is for the whole of humanity.[1]

[When you have this quality,] you are generous, you are hospitable, you are friendly and caring and compassionate. You share what you

---

1. Desmond Tutu, AZ Quotes website, https://www.azquotes.com/quote/926180.

have. It is to say, "My humanity is inextricably bound up in yours." We belong in a bundle of life.—Archbishop Desmond Tutu[2]

Statelessness and *Ubuntu*

Many Southern Africans have heard the story that goes something like this: "In the old days when we were young, a traveller through a country would stop at a village, and he didn't have to ask for food or water; once he stops, the people give him food, entertain him."[3]

That is one aspect of *Ubuntu* that emphasizes the humanity of every individual, regardless of their social status. A traveller was seen as a human person worthy of hospitality and was not reduced to their social status of outsider. A significant concern many have toward this welcoming and generous attitude is resources. Can a society that continuously recognizes and welcomes travellers and meets their needs thrive economically?

The hospitality of *Ubuntu* was never meant to impoverish host societies. Put succinctly, as we seek to secure ourselves materially, *Ubuntu* asks us, "Are you also doing so to improve the lives of those in your community? And to those who do not belong because they are considered outsiders?" As Christians, we know that several Bible passages are clear on hospitality as a virtue. For instance, one of the harshest consequences for the ill treatment of travellers is found in Genesis 19, where God struck blind those who plotted harm against Lot's guests and destroyed their city.

Few stateless people are travellers. There is a diversity in statelessness. For instance, while some are migrants, others inherit a stateless status and are likely to pass it on to their children if policies remain unchanged. Despite the range of ways statelessness is manifested, many view stateless people as travellers who are temporarily stuck in a country on their way elsewhere. Stateless people usually are not just passing through. By definition, they do not belong

---

2. Kate Torgovnick May, "I am, because of you: Further reading on Ubuntu," TEDblog (9 December 2013), quoting Desmond Tutu, https://blog.ted.com/further-reading-on-ubuntu.

3. May, "I am, because of you," quoting Nelson Mandela.

anywhere as citizens, yet they need to live their lives where they are. I believe our call as church communities is to recognize the injustice of this liminal space of statelessness. This call is in line with the resolutions made at the 10th Assembly of the World Council of Churches (WCC) in Busan, Republic of Korea, in 2013. There, in response to the plight of stateless people around the world, the WCC resolved that it:

A. **Affirms** that the right to life, security and basic human rights are fundamental universal principles and values that every human being is entitled to;

B. **Recognizes** that the denial of nationality is a major violation of human rights which affects people in every region;

C. **Encourages** churches to raise awareness of the situation of stateless people living in their countries and around the world and to advocate for the protection of their human rights;

D. **Calls** on churches to engage in dialogue with states to adopt policies which confer nationality and provide proper documentation to state-less people;

E. **Acknowledges** positive changes in nationality laws made by some governments, and encourages other states to take similar actions;

F. **Urges** churches, civil society, human rights entities as well as United Nations agencies and regional organizations to collaborate in order to properly and effectively reduce and eradicate statelessness;

G. **Prays** for stateless people around the world, so that their voices are heard and their plight understood; and

H. **Requests** the WCC to take up the issue of stateless people as one of its programmatic priorities until the forthcoming WCC 11th Assembly.[4]

In the light of the points above, and in dialogue with biblical passages like Philippians 2:1-4, let us also consider how the values of *Ubuntu* can inform and deepen our Christian reflection on statelessness.

---

4. World Council of Churches, "Statement on the Human Rights of Stateless People" (2013), https://www.oikoumene.org/sites/default/files/Document/PIC%2002_2%20ADOPTED%20Human%20Rights%20of%20Stateless%20People.pdf.

Ubuntu and *Imago Dei*

Ubuntu is a Nguni (Ndebele/Zulu/Xhosa) word that can be translated into English as "humanness" and how humanness informs being humane. The term *Ubuntu* has parallels in many other African languages and societies: for instance, it is *umunthu* in Chichewa (Malawi), *hunhu* in Shona (Zimbabwe), *umuntu* in Bemba (Zambia), and so on. It is a people-centred philosophy — an African concept of the individual in relationship with others in the community and society.[5] In other words, it is a collection of values and practices that guide people's interactions as authentic human beings who are, from the perspective of *Ubuntu*, "part of a larger and more significant relational, communal, societal, environmental and spiritual world."[6] This has been summarized in popular maxims such as "I am because we are" or "A person is a person through other people." *Ubuntu* has come under increasing strain over time as African societies change and adapt to the demands and challenges of the 21st century.[7] However, it remains an ideal that, when practised, can provide some more humane (and more just) approaches to challenges that our societies face today.

Concerning statelessness, the idea of interconnectedness in *Ubuntu* emphasizes the need to recognize that stateless people's humanity is bound in our humanity. Furthermore, the *Ubuntu* maxim "I am because you are" seems to affirm the theological motif of *imago Dei*. When we see each human being as created in the image of God, we recognize that stateless people should be treated with equal dignity as brothers and sisters and fellow

---

5. Mennas Vincent Mukaka, "Meaning of Umunthu: Community Spirit for the Building of the Human Community on the Example of the Socio-Political Situation of Malawi," PhD diss., Karl-Franzens University of Graz, 2015, https://unipub.uni-graz.at/obvugrhs/content/titleinfo/757384/full.pdf.

6. Jacob Rugare Mugumbate and Admire Chereni, "Editorial: Now, the Theory of Ubuntu Has Its Space in Social Work," *African Journal of Social Work* 10:1 (2020), v, https://www.ajol.info/index.php/ajsw/article/view/195112.

7. See, for example, Fredrick Golooba-Mutebi, *"Don't look for Ubuntu here, modern lifestyles eroded it,"* *The East African*, 20 April 2018, https://www.theeastafrican.co.ke/tea/oped/comment/don-t-look-for-ubuntu-here-modern-lifestyles-eroded-it--1389872.

image-bearers. In other words, *Ubuntu* and *imago Dei* provide us with an ethic to see stateless people as fellow image-bearers and, in solidarity with them, advocate for justice. Some practical ways we can achieve this include basing our ethics of statelessness on "human dignity, equality, universal brotherhood, sacredness of life and community life."[8] This, in turn, pushes the church worldwide to look for ways that ensure stateless people can holistically belong in our communities (socially), countries (the human right to citizenship), faith communities (spiritually), and so on.

As the church worldwide, we should be troubled when people are denied their human right to formally belong and to enjoy the privileges that belonging in a society entails. Philippians 2:1-4 provides us with some lessons that we can consider. I find the *Africa Bible Commentary*'s interpretation of this passage useful to our discussion on statelessness. Apart from the passage's obvious focus on the Philippian Christian community and its challenges, the Commentary highlights for us the key issues of humility and concern for others in the spirit of *Ubuntu*. Thus, the Commentary's comments on Philippians 2:3-4 includes the following statement:

> Those who claim to follow Christ should have concern for the community as well as for themselves. True Christians should have a "body" mindset, the mindset of togetherness. Their attitude should be close to that expressed in Africa as "I am, because we are", though for Christians this statement should reflect the reality that Christ is in the believer, rather than being merely a cultural philosophy.[9]

In the light of the statement above, let us explore Philippians 2:1-4 further. By looking at the passage as an ethical model, we can use it in dialogue with *Ubuntu* in response to the issue of statelessness.

---

8. Mukaka, "Meaning of Umunthu," 5.

9. See "Philippians 2:1-4: The Right Attitude," in *Africa Bible Commentary: A One-Volume Commentary Written by 70 African Scholars*, ed. Tokunboh Adeyemo (Nairobi: WordAlive, 2010), 1442.

Philippians 2:1-4 as an Ethical Model

Philippians 2:1-4 gives an opportunity to consider several key themes. Verse 1 contains the implied question "Has Christ ever been gentle and loving toward you?" Although we may all have different responses to this question, some fundamental Christian theological doctrines compel us to acknowledge that Christ's mission on earth and his dying on the cross were his expression of love to us. His gentleness is highlighted throughout his earthly ministry and best summarized, perhaps, in the metaphor of the good shepherd (John 10:14-18). As such, his love draws our attention to verse 2, "hav[e] the same love." Granted, Paul was addressing the Philippian Christians in the context of their fellowship as believers, as we read in the rest of the passage. However, we can apply this call not only to our homes, churches, and communities, but also, specifically, to the invisible and the marginalized among us. The call to love sums up all the commandments: we are to love God and our neighbour (Matt. 22:37-40), and love and gentleness are both the fruit of the Holy Spirit (Gal. 5:22-23).

Furthermore, love is meant to be active and practical: in other words, "according to Scripture, love has form and content and it compels us to act. . . . (1 Cor. 13; Matt 5:43-47)."[10] The authors continue, ""Loving our neighbors involves actively seeking their wellbeing." Therefore, we do not love the marginalized among us just so we can feel good about ourselves; rather, we love so we can serve them. What does this look like in your community? Can you or your church community do more to advocate for the rights of stateless people around the world? Can you do more to be a welcoming church for stateless people? Can you contribute more positively to their welfare? Philippians 2:3-4 seems to give us some guidelines as we respond to these questions and more:

> Do nothing from selfish ambition or conceit, but in humility regard others as better than yourselves. Let each of you look not to your own interests, but to the interests of others.

---

10. Justin Giboney, Michael Wear, and Chris Butler, *Compassion (&) Conviction: The AND Campaign's Guide to Faithful Civic Engagement* (Westmont, IL: InterVarsity Press, 2020), 9, https://ivpress.org/Media/Default/Downloads/Excerpts-and-Samples/4810-excerpt.pdf.

Now that an ethical model has been suggested, let us consider a more just concept of "citizenship/nationality."

A More Just Concept of "Nationality": The Right to Have Rights

According to the United Nations High Commissioner for Refugees (UNHCR), nationality is a human right. It is also enshrined in Article 15 of the 1948 Universal Declaration of Human Rights. This means that all countries that follow this Declaration affirm that every individual in the world has the right to a legal connection with a state. They affirm that:

> Citizenship or nationality (the two terms are used interchangeably [by the UNHCR], just as they are in international law) not only provides people with a sense of identity, it entitles individuals to the protection of a State and to many civil and political rights. Indeed, citizenship has been described as "the right to have rights.[11]"[12]

However, these affirmations have not translated well into policies. There are an estimated 15 million stateless people worldwide.[13] It is difficult to get exact figures because less than half of the world's countries submit data.[14] The available data accounts for 4.2 million people,[15] which indicates that anywhere between at least 4.2 and 15 million people have no "right to have rights." Our call, then, based on our love for (Phil. 2:1-4) stateless people and our recognition of their humanity (*Ubuntu*), is to join in solidarity with

---

11. "Citizenship is man's basic right for it is nothing less than the right to have rights." Item 39, Chief Justice Earl Warren (USA 1958). *Clemente Martinez PEREZ, Petitioner, v. Herbert BROWNELL, Jr., Attorney General of the United States of America,* https://www.law.cornell.edu/supremecourt/text/356/44.

12. Interparliamentary Union with the UNHCR, *Nationality and Statelessness: A Handbook for Parliamentarians* n° 11, Interparliamentary Union (Geneva: IPU, 2005), 3.

13. Institute on Statelessness and Inclusion, "Statelessness in Numbers: 2020: An Overview and Analysis of Global Statistics," August 2020, https://files.institutesi.org/ISI_statistics_analysis_2020.pdf.

14. Ibid.

15. Ibid.

efforts to attain their right to have rights. This goes beyond the call to be welcoming as a church. It includes being aware that this is a human rights issue and is attainable when states act on their affirmation of these rights. Considering that many people are unaccounted for, it is difficult for the church to address statelessness in practical ways on a case-by-case basis alone. It is a global problem that needs our solidarity, with interventions at the individual and policy levels. To put this into perspective, let us consider the story of Ruth.[16] This fictional story brings together several challenges that stateless people have shared. It shows some limits that local churches can face even when trying to help stateless people at the individual level only.

Ruth's Story

Immigration officers stopped Ruth on her way from work. She did not have her papers on her. In fact, she had no papers. Her mother had arrived in the country as a pregnant young woman fleeing the political instability in her home country. When she arrived in her new, safe "home," she breathed a sigh of relief. She had crossed over by foot with no documents to prove who she was or where she came from and learned to keep her head down. She did not want to risk being deported. She worked odd jobs. When her daughter, Ruth, was born, she taught Ruth how to keep her head down too. But now Ruth was being taken to a detention centre for "illegal immigrants."

They asked about her ID. She had none. Birth certificate? None. Her mother had delivered her in a rural health centre near the border town where she had gotten her first job. They asked Ruth where she came from; they wanted to know where to deport her. She had no idea. She knew nothing about where her mother had come from. All she knew was the bustling community of the city where she had grown up. Her friends were here. Her old school was here. She worked here. She was part of the community, as her mother had been. Her mother hardly ever spoke about where she had come from. She made vague mention of ethnic tension and her escape through several countries to get here,

---

16. This fictional story has been written to highlight actual experiences of stateless people that have been made public through the media.

but nothing more. She had never wanted to talk about it, so she had learned the local language, the local norms and customs, and had passed them on to Ruth.

Her mother's church community was the strongest community around her. When her mother died suddenly, the church gave her a dignified funeral. She had belonged, and it had not mattered to them that she had national roots elsewhere.

Now Ruth wondered if that community could help her get out of this detention centre. Surely they had many records of her existence – her baptism certificate, her church's elementary and high school IDs. Surely the church would help. She was a choir member, a Sunday school teacher, and a volunteer at many church events. She was what one would call "a member in good standing," just as her mother had been. She mentioned this to the case officer, who told her right away that these documents were not enough. "This means you are stateless. You don't belong anywhere," he said. "What does that mean?" Ruth asked. He explained that a stateless person is someone not recognized as a citizen by any country. She asked if she could become a citizen, seeing as she was born here. She was told there was no legislation that gave her that right. The days passed. Many interviews with her case officer later, Ruth realized she could do nothing but wait. Maybe they would try and figure out where her mother had come from. What then? She did not know. She had to wait.

Ruth's story highlights how people who are stateless are denied the right to belong or to have their human rights protected. They participate socio-religiously, socio-economically, and socio-culturally in our communities but are not legally guaranteed the rights and privileges others have. We can do more to advocate for changing this status quo.

Final Thoughts: The Right to Have Rights as *Ubuntu* in Dialogue with Philippians 2:1-4

Philippians 2:3 reminds us: "Do nothing from selfish ambition." This should prompt us to be troubled when one group gets an advantage based on their social status or citizenship/nationality and other groups do not. Are we willingly getting ahead while those who are stateless are denied their rights? And how can we do better? I believe that joining in solidarity with them as they fight for the right to belong – the right to have rights – is in the spirit of *Ubuntu*: "I am because you are." It conveys to them the sense that we are each part of "a larger whole whose wellbeing depends on every member's wellbeing."[17] We can translate this idea for this cause into "I belong because you belong." It is also in line with passages like Philippians 2:1-4, whose call is to look out for the good of others and to value them in humility, love, and gentleness. For this cause, this translates into life-giving, not life-denying, action, in solidarity with people who are stateless – at the individual level but also in advocacy. In this, may we have *Ubuntu* that is – to echo Archbishop Tutu's words noted above – generous, hospitable, friendly, caring, and compassionate. Sharing what we have. Saying, "'My humanity is inextricably bound up in yours.' We belong in a bundle of life."

---

17. Golooba-Mutebi, *"Don't look for Ubuntu here."*

CHAPTER 3

A (FAKA)ALOFA / STRANGER FROM TUVALU: THE FUTURE OF CLIMATE CHANGE–DISPLACED PEOPLES*

MAINA TALIA

"Which one of you, having a hundred sheep and losing one of them, does not leave the ninety-nine in the wilderness and go after the one that is lost until he finds it?" (Luke 15:4)

Oge pati: Lost for Words

It is not easy to talk about statelessness in Tuvalu. There are number of reasons for this difficulty. One of the most obvious has to do with there being no Indigenous word for it. That should come as no surprise. This lack of a word stems from a difference in conceptual worldviews. The very idea of being stateless is strange to the Indigenous worldview of a (relatively still) integrated traditional society like those found on the eight low-lying islands that make up the sovereign nation of Tuvalu. The word—and the concept—comes from international law. Here it presupposes a lack or loss of nationality which would otherwise be acquired by birth or by descent. It is possible for a citizen to revoke their nationality, but, according to the United Nations'

---

*Parts of this paper was published by the author on https://www.researchgate.net/publication/342407360_MIGRATION_IS_A_DEFINITE_NO_BUT_RATHER_A_MATTER_OF_CHOICE_VOICE_FROM_THE_MARGIN declaration on refugees (to which Tuvalu is a signatory), not if it renders the person stateless.

In the absence of an Indigenous word, the default practice is to use the English (*gana palagi*) equivalent. It could be argued that the nearest customary usage has to do with the practice of banishment – *fakafolau*. This word means "to sail away, to be sent into exile." It presumes an act of violation that will bring shame (*fakalumagina*) and disgrace to the whole community. The person is removed from the heart of the family and the community. The one who is banished is set adrift in a canoe that is filled with holes. The most likely outcome is death. The custom remains in a modified form. Those who do not comply with what is required will be sent away by the *kaiga aliki* (the chiefly institution) to live on another island, without the right to return.

This lack of a word to do with statelessness is not surprising in another sense, as well. The way of life emphasizes participation, kinship, and belonging. The intimate and close connection with the land is embodied through the placenta (*fanua*) being buried on the island (*fenua*) upon which one has been born. The symbolism of this rite is that the individual always belongs. It is thus unlike a category of citizenship which can be revoked, with the person running the risk of becoming stateless.

That becomes clear when we take a closer look at how this society functions under the power of *aliki* (chiefs): it is they who decide what is best for the community. On Vaitupu, my island, a man is qualified to speak in the *falekaupule* (traditional meeting place) on the condition that he has or represents a *mataniu*.[1] This traditional concept of *mataniu* directly links us to land: land is sacred and, in Pacific countries, "tends to have meanings to those who 'belong' to or are 'part of it' that are often difficult to encapsulate

---

1. *Mataniu* – literally means "coconut's face." Contextually, it refers to a man who has been appointed to be the head of the family; he takes on a special role in serving their *aliki* (chiefs) and takes care of all family lands and *pulaka* pits. Personal conversation with Talia M. Salasopa at Vaitupu, 18 February 2019.

in English or other colonial languages."[2] Many Tuvaluan words describe land: *fenua, fanua, laukele, manafa, potu, nuku,* and *tia. Fanua*'s literal meaning is equivalent to the word "placenta,"[3] which is spelled slightly different from the word *fenua,* but with parallel meaning.[4] Through cultural practices that are reflected in our languages, we are culturally bonded to the land: this bond is not easily disregarded. This land is the same land in which our ancestors are laid to rest; if we are to leave, we must take them with us.

The other side of this coin is how our people are a "seawater people." The *moana* (the sea) also plays a vital role in our lives. Our main diet is fish; a meal without *mea ota* (raw fish) is not a Tuvaluan meal! The seashores are looked upon as playing fields for our young ones. They play freely and unsupervised; there are no life guards to watch over them, for they know how to live with the sea. That is why moving to much larger countries, especially those that are landlocked, is so unbearable. We need to be next to the sea, which is a source of living for us.

The concept of being stateless is also difficult to comprehend due to how our cultures respond to the one who is without a home. The keyword here is *fakaalofa,* which has two meanings. The first has to with being a stranger — that is, a person without any land rights. The second conveys a sense of being

---

2. John Campbell, "Climate-induced Community Relocation in the Pacific: The Meaning and Importance of Land," in *Climate Change and Displacement: Multidisciplinary Perspectives,* ed. Jane McAdam (London: Hart, 2010), 60.

3. The coconut will always be the tree planted on top of the placenta, which is called *niu-fakamauganiu,* or *tena inu,* meaning that this coconut will provide drinks for the child — a source of life. The placenta is normally buried, but the umbilical cord will be either buried or thrown into the sea. This custom is done with a wish that, when the child grows up, the child will become a good fisherman or a good planter. Note that the Samoans also use the same word to refer to the placenta and land. See Ama'amalele Tofaeono, *Eco-theology: Aiga- The Household of Life* (Neuendettelsau: Freimund-Druckerei, 2009), 181. In the Fijian context, the umbilical cord of a boy will be buried, while that of the girls will be thrown to the ocean. See, Josefa Mairara, "The Floating Coconut: A Contextual Approach to Methodist Mission in Fiji," *Asia Journal of Theology* 21:2 (2007), 187.

4. Tapugao Falefou, *Toku Tia: Tuvalu and the Impacts of Climate Change,* PhD diss., Waikato University, 2017, 144.

unfortunate, pitiable, hopeless. It speaks to the affections and emotions. The best description of a *fakalofa* is reflected in the story of the good Samaritan who showed compassion to the man on the road to Jericho who had been set upon by robbers.

There is an irony attached to this situation. The possibility of a whole people becoming stateless presumes a policy of leaving the land that makes up that nation. To this day, the government of Tuvalu does not have a plan B that would cover this scenario. To date, there has been no community-based discussion on whether such a plan is necessary. The prospect of having to leave the islands is deemed to be a matter of personal choice. The reason that there is no plan B is partly the desire not to send the wrong signals to a global audience, to give the impression that our people are willing to relocate. A plan B might lead other states to wonder, "Why bother with the fate of doomed low-lying islands?"

There are reasons behind the desire not to speak of being stateless which have to do with geopolitical strategy as well as how climate justice (and responsibility) plays out. In his role as the foreign affairs permanent secretary, the Hon. Sopoaga was afraid that if the country's very existence is questioned, there is a risk: such a policy might generate the view that adaptation is pointless and could have a negative impact on foreign aid.[5] The fate of the nation must not be determined by foreign aid or a political agenda, but by a concern for the safety of the nation.

Not having a plan B and seeing the decision to leave as a personal choice also resonate with theological conviction. There may not be any sheep on Tuvalu, but the parable Jesus tells of the one that is lost speaks. What if that sheep represents the one who stays? Are they now a *fakalofa* or are they *faitonu* (stubborn)? On the basis of our Indigenous wisdom (*muna o te fale*) and faith, what are we to do if only one of us does not want to leave his *fenua* (island), his parents' resting place, and the place where his or her *fanua* (placenta) is buried?

---

5. Jane McAdam, *Climate Change, Forced Migration and International Law* (Oxford: Oxford University Press, 2012), 34.

Kaia fua nei? Why Talk about Being Stateless Now?

There is also a more contemporary reluctance to use the word "stateless." It has to do with rising sea levels, global warming, climate change, and the sustainability of terrestrial life on the ancestral lands. Will our islands be overcome by the sea and our inhabitants become climate-displaced persons?[6] The issues are complex and evolving. There is a need to proceed with care. Some definitions and distinctions need to be made.

The first has to do with how the line is to be drawn between migration and relocation when it comes to the climate narrative. The Inter-agency Network for Education in Emergencies provides this definition for migration:

> The movement of a person or a group of persons, either across an international border, or within a State. It is a population movement, encompassing any kind of movement of people, whatever its length, composition and causes; it includes migration of refugees, displaced persons, economic migrants, and persons moving for other purposes, including family reunification.[7]

This definition clearly contends that migration is an activity that individuals and households undertake[8]; this activity may happen internally or externally. It does not require any approval from a larger group or from the

---

6. We are not only observing rising seas during high tides, but also the bubbling up of seawater from the ground. The detrended pattern of rainfall will pose a great challenge to the agriculture sector, as it will disturb our traditionally stable root crops and livestock, forcing our people to rely heavily on imported foods for survival. Cyclones cause many internal displacements. One example happened in March 2015. Tuvalu was severely hit by tropical cyclone Pam, forcing 71 families (40 percent of the population) of Nui Island to relocate further inland because of severe storm surges that unearthed multiple graves, exposing bones and human remains. One hundred percent of the vegetation, including traditional crops, was affected, as the waves seeped through the whole island and lasted for almost a day. Such terrifying situations raise the question of why there is a delay in putting forth a plan B for Tuvalu to ensure full security while worst-case scenarios are already being encountered.

7. Inter-agency Network for Education in Emergencies, "Glossary" (2021), https://inee.org/eie-glossary/migration

8. Falefou, *Toku Tia*, 238.

community. Migration is a matter of individual movement. John Campbell defines relocation as:

> the permanent (or long-term) movement of a community (or a significant part of it) from one location to another, in which important characteristics of the original community, including its social structures, legal and political systems, cultural characteristics and worldviews are retained; the community stays together at the destination in a social form that is similar to the community of origin.[9]

Relocation has distinct elements and characteristics: it is an organized movement of people done in a highly facilitated way. It requires much preparation for it to be accomplished in a timely manner. It must be done in a way that ensures that the rights and aspirations of a relocated people are well recognized and respected by the receiving country or countries.

Relocation raises the spectre of statelessness in a way which migration does not and generates discordant responses. The likelihood of climate-induced displacement led the Hon. Teleke Peleti to declare during Conference of the Parties (COP)6 (2000) that "[t]his concern is so serious for our people, that the cabinet, in which I am a member, has been exploring the possibility of buying land in a nearby country, in case we become refugees [due] to the impacts of climate change."[10]

That scenario stands alongside this call made in 2008 and 2009 by then prime minister Apisai Ielemia:

> While Tuvalu faces an uncertain future because of climate change, it is our view that Tuvaluans will remain in Tuvalu. We will fight to keep our country, our culture and our way of living. We are not considering any migration scheme. We believe if the right actions are taken to address climate change, Tuvalu will survive.[11]

---

9. Campbell, "Climate-Induced Community Relocation in the Pacific," 58–59.

10. Statement by the Hon. Teleke P. Lauti at COP6 (The Hague, November 2000), cited in UNFCC, *Climate Change: Small Island Developing States* (Climate Change Secretariat, 2005), 13. Cited in McAdam, *Climate Change, Forced Migration and International Law*, 144.

11. McAdam, *Climate Change, Forced Migration and International Law*, 35.

International law recognizes only a very small class of forced migrants as people whom other countries have an obligation to protect: refugees, stateless persons, and those eligible for complementary protection.[12] In the absence of any international law that accommodates people displaced by climate change, the prime minister of Tuvalu, the Rt Hon. Enele S. Sopoaga, has emphasized that the "current refugee regimes … do not adequately protect people forced to leave their homes by the impacts of climate change."[13] He proposed a United Nations resolution to establish a legal process to protect the human rights and lives of those displaced by climate change.[14] This matter is a priority for the Government of Tuvalu to ensure that when the time comes, we are fully protected and safe.

There is much doubt that the international community will respond positively to our proposal. The United Kingdom and countries comprising the European Union are not inclined to accept our proposal, as it will open the floodgates for millions of people who are qualified to be called climate victims. The proposal for protecting those who are affected by climate change is not, after all, confined to Tuvalu. It crosses borders. Under such circumstances, international legal protection is developed and discussed primarily for climate-induced migration caused by natural disasters and acute emergencies. It barely considers that climate-induced migration should ideally be based on a voluntary, early, and self-determined decision.[15]

---

12. Jane McAdam, "Climate Change Displacement and International Law: Side Event to the High Commissioner's Dialogue on Protection Challenges," 8 December 2010, Geneva, 3, https://www.refworld.org/pdfid/4d95a1532.pdf. See McAdam, *Climate Change, Forced Migration and International Law*, 43.

13. "Statement Presented by the Prime Minister of Tuvalu, Honourable Enele Sosene Sopoaga, The 72nd Session of the United Nations General Assembly General Debate, September 17, 2017, New York," https://gadebate.un.org/sites/default/files/gastatements/72/tv_en.pdf.

14. General Assembly of the United Nations, 21 September 2017, https://gadebate.un.org/en/72/tuvalu.

15. German Advisory Council on Global Change, *Just & In-Time Climate Policy: Four Initiatives for a Fair Transformation*, Climate Policy Paper no. 9, August 2018, 26.

Dealing with international law makes it important to discuss the term "climate change refugees": where does such talk fit into the discussion? The 1951 Refugee Convention relating to the Status of Refugees, read in conjunction with its 1967 Protocol, defines refugees in these words:

> owing to wellfounded fear of being persecuted for reasons of race, religion, nationality, membership of a particular social group or political opinion, is outside the country of his nationality and is unable or, owing to such fear, is unwilling to avail himself of the protection of that country; or who, not having a nationality and being outside the country of his former habitual residence as a result of such events, is unable or, owing to such fear, is unwilling to return to it.[16]

McAdam points out two major obstacles that make it difficult for people displaced by the impacts of climate change to be regarded as refugees within the meaning of the Convention. First, it applies to those who have crossed international borders; second, it is difficult to characterize climate change as persecution—although she found the argument to be unconvincing because "persecution entails violation of human rights."[17] In a number of cases in Australia and New Zealand, people from Tuvalu and Kiribati have sought litigation, arguing that they should receive refugee protection on the basis of climate change: no case has been successful.[18] Clearly, the court did not want to set a precedent. There is another side to this business: none of us from the Pacific wants to be labelled a climate change refugee, as it takes away the essence of our pride in being a Pacific Islander. Anote Tong, the former president of Kiribati, expressed this sentiment: "when you talk about refugees—climate refugees—you're putting the stigma on the victims, not the offenders."[19] During the Climate Change Induced Migration workshop hosted by Tuvalu Associations of non-governmental organizations in partnership with

---

16. United Nations, Refugee Convention (n 12), Article 1A(2), https://www.unhcr.org/4ae57b489.pdf.

17. McAdam, "The Relevance of International Refugee Law," 42–43.

18. McAdam, *Climate Change, Forced Migration and International Law*, 43.

19. Ibid., 41.

the Unitarian Universalist Service Committee, participants preferred the term "climate forced displacement" over the term "climate forced migrants," as the latter carries the stigma of being a migrant.[20]

Of equal complexity and ambiguity in matters of international law is the question of statehood. What happens if a state is subject to its entire disappearance? To qualify as a state, it is required under international law, as provided for in the Montevideo Convention on the Rights and Duties of States, to have the following: "(a) a permanent population, (b) a defined territory, (c) government, and (d) a capacity to enter into relations with the other states."[21] Tuvalu is obviously on the verge of losing these fundamental principles that qualify us to be called a state. Iakoba Taeia Italeli, the governor general of Tuvalu, asked in his academic thesis "whether such a State [like Tuvalu] could continue to exist as a State if its total land area is covered by sea or so much of it that it cannot sustain sufficient population to have an economic life of its own."[22] No international law exists to provide sufficient answers when an island is completely submerged.

Our greatest fear has to do with what happens if Tuvalu disappears. Who will have ownership of this exclusive economic zone (EEZ)? Can Tuvaluans relocate and still have ownership of their EEZ and airspace? Or does this issue need to be determined by powerful countries? For Simon Kofe, "the question really is whether the principle of continuity can be applied to Tuvalu, if it loses its territory, remains to be seen. The lack of precedent in such cases leaves the matter open for interpretation with States ultimately deciding whether or not to recognize the sovereignty of such States."[23]

---

20. "Climate Change Induced Displacement" (unpublished report from the workshop "Toku Fenua, Toku Tofi: My Island, My Birthright," Tuvalu Association of Non-Governmental Organizations [TANGO], Funafuti, Tuvalu, June 21–22, 2018).

21. Montevideo Convention on the Rights and Duties of States (1933), art. 1, https://www .jus.uio.no/english/services/library/treaties/01/1-02/rights-duties-states.xml.

22. Iakoba Taeia Italeli, "The Legal Aspects of Sea Level Rise on Maritime Boundaries Pertaining to Low-lying Coastal and Island States: An Island Perspective," LLM thesis, International Maritime Law Institute, Malta, 2001, 41.

23. Simon Kofe, "The Legal Implications of Climate Change on the Statehood of Tuvalu," LLM thesis, International Maritime Law Institute, Malta, 2014, 16.

Look Who's Talking

The word "stateless" is relatively new to the peoples of Tuvalu. It carries a sense of urgency and threat. Its arrival in Tuvalu with regard to the changing climate was most likely associated with the workshop on climate change–induced displacement held at Kainaki Falekaupule in Funafuti on 21-22 June 2018. The workshop, organized by the Tuvalu Association of Non-Governmental Organisations (TANGO), met under the prophetic theme of *Toku Fenua Toku Tofi* (My Island, My Birthright). The panel for the occasion was selected with the purpose of generating discussion on "the need to promote and protect traditional knowledge, the implications of climate change on statehood, the economic and noneconomic loss and damage caused by climate change, and the role of the church and international law."[24]

In his opening remarks, Rev. Tafue Lusama, president of TANGO, expressed the importance of differentiating between the "free will migration of individuals and mass relocations of peoples."[25] This distinction lay behind the counsel of the prime minister, Enele Sopoaga, who emphasized the human rights of those adversely affected by climate change and the need for legal protection. Sopoaga referred to "induced displacement for a safe and secure future"; this basic stance was qualified by the common desire to view relocation as "the final option" for the peoples of Tuvalu. It was a position that was accompanied by the recognized importance of preserving cultural identity for a potentially displaced nation through its "cultural and traditional values."

The workshop took a rights-based approach to climate change and its impacts on a vulnerable nation. Tuvalu was deemed to be part of the international family and as such required international cooperation and assistance to deal with a problem not of its own making. In other parts of the world, the

---

24. Seforosa Carroll, "Too Late for Justice?" in *Christian Theology in the Age of Migration: Implications for World Christianity*, ed. Peter C. Phan (London: Rowman & Littlefield, 2020), 227.

25. "Climate Change Induced Displacement" (unpublished report from the workshop "Toku Fenua, Toku Tofi: My Island, My Birthright," Tuvalu Association of Non-Governmental Organizations [TANGO], Funafuti, Tuvalu, June 21–22, 2018).

plight of Tuvalu may not be so well known, but this workshop was sensitive to the global discussions arising out of the Paris Agreement[26] as well as the Global Compact for Migration[27] and the New York Declaration for Refugees and Migrants[28].

Ghazali Ohorella, an international law and Indigenous rights expert, situated the future of displaced peoples within the ambit of the UN Declaration on the Rights of Indigenous Peoples[29]. The former president of Kiribati, Antone Tong, sought to put a human face – that of the wellbeing of future generations – on a problem (climate change) that had often been discussed in overly scientific, or abstract terms. The sheer seriousness of the cultural situation was captured by Simon Kofe, senior magistrate of Tuvalu. The particular issues he addressed concerned the implications of climate change on statehood, sovereignty, and "the potential absence of a physical territory or population[30]." For Tapugao Falefou, the overriding concern was the intersection of identity with sovereignty.

The workshop produced an Outcome Document. It referred to the people being "indigenous to our islands"; it identified how "the unforgiving impacts of climate change" will "negatively transform our society as a whole." It spoke most directly to the "fear of the loss of our ancestral lands will force us into extinction." [31] The Outcome Document was clear about how climate change has "exacerbate[d] the challenges and disadvantages already faced by Indigenous Peoples in the Pacific[32]" and left these nations in a position of

---

26. The Paris Agreement (2015) https://unfccc.int/process-and-meetings/the-paris-agreement/the-paris-agreement.

27. The Global Compact for Migration (2018), https://www.iom.int/global-compact-migration.

28. Ibid.

29. UN Declaration on the Rights of Indigenous Peoples (2007), https://www.un.org/development/desa/indigenouspeoples/declaration-on-the-rights-of-indigenous-peoples.html.

30. Climate Change Induced Displacement" (unpublished report from the workshop "Toku Fenua, Toku Tofi: My Island, My Birthright," Tuvalu Association of Non-Governmental Organizations [TANGO], Funafuti, Tuvalu, June 21–22, 2018).

31. Ibid.

32. Ibid.

political and economic marginalization. The Outcome Document concluded with a set of commitments gathered around the need to stand "for what is right and best for our Peoples[33]." The option of migration induced by climate change was deemed to be "the last resort," to be considered only after "all options and avenues available to us" have been "exhausted[34]."

The language of statelessness was not used in the final document coming out of this workshop. It was nevertheless used in meeting itself — and, indeed, was implied throughout the conversation to do with induced migration, sovereignty, the preservation of culture and "existence."[35] Within this context of low-lying islands in an "age of climate change,"[36] statelessness means something quite different from those who are stateless due to being a refugee or an outcast from a state that is caught up in an external war or internal civil strife. The experience and the future possibilities are not necessarily the same: the UN Conventions on the Reduction of Statelessness of 1954 and 1961 did not envisage climate-induced statelessness.

"Are You Not My Neighbour?"

This Outcome Document represents a summary of the threats to land, identity, sovereignty, worldview, Indigenous customs, and knowledge. It conveys tragedy and reflects how a moral storm affects a society noted for its subsistence emissions. It is the voice of a weak actor in the current geopolitics of climate change. Only a handful of nations around the globe face the radical nature of statelessness the way Tuvalu does. It is the kind of situation which invites a moral claim: the parable of the good Samaritan invites those who live beyond the *tautologa* horizon of our islands to consider our question to you: "Am I not your neighbour? Am I not your *tuakoi?*"

---

33. Ibid

34. Ibid.

35. Ibid.

36. Ibid.

CHAPTER 4

"OUTSIDERS":
A DEVOTIONAL REFLECTION ON GENDER EQUALITY AND STATELESSNESS[*]

KELLI D. JOLLY

The child grew, and was weaned; and Abraham made a great feast on the day that Isaac was weaned. But Sarah saw the son of Hagar the Egyptian, whom she had borne to Abraham, playing with her son Isaac. So she said to Abraham, "Cast out this slave woman with her son; for the son of this slave woman shall not inherit along with my son Isaac." The matter was very distressing to Abraham on account of his son. But God said to Abraham, "Do not be distressed because of the boy and because of your slave woman; whatever Sarah says to you, do as she tells you, for it is through Isaac that offspring shall be named after you. As for the son of the slave woman, I will make a nation of him also, because he is your offspring." So Abraham rose early in the morning, and took bread and a skin of water, and gave it to Hagar, putting it on her shoulder, along with the child, and sent her away. And she departed, and wandered about in the wilderness of Beer-sheba.

When the water in the skin was gone, she cast the child under one of the bushes. Then she went and sat down opposite him a good way off,

---

*This paper is based on a WCC workshop held in Curaçao in 2018.

about the distance of a bowshot; for she said, "Do not let me look on the death of the child." And as she sat opposite him, she lifted up her voice and wept. And God heard the voice of the boy; and the angel of God called to Hagar from heaven, and said to her, "What troubles you, Hagar? Do not be afraid; for God has heard the voice of the boy where he is. Come, lift up the boy and hold him fast with your hand, for I will make a great nation of him." Then God opened her eyes, and she saw a well of water. She went, and filled the skin with water, and gave the boy a drink.

God was with the boy, and he grew up; he lived in the wilderness, and became an expert with the bow. He lived in the wilderness of Paran; and his mother got a wife for him from the land of Egypt. (Gen. 21:8-21)

Case 1

Ricardo is an unmarried Bahamian man who has a child with a foreign woman. When she enquired about obtaining a passport for the child in the Bahamas so the child could be baptized, his proud Bahamian grandmother was told outright that the child was not eligible for citizenship because the child was born outside the Bahamas to a woman to whom her son was not married.

Case 2

Brittney's father is Bahamian born. She was born to a single woman outside of the Bahamas. Because of the Bahamas' citizenship laws, her father could not automatically pass on his citizenship. She is now an adult with emotional, historical, and cultural ties to a country where she is not entitled to any citizenship rights. She has been denied a driver's license, a bank account, an updated National Insurance Board card, and vehicle registration. She visits the Bahamas regularly for as long as the Immigration Department will allow, but because of these experiences and others, she says that she continues to be treated as an outsider.

•   •   •

An "outsider": That is how Brittney in Case 2 describes herself. Although she is not stateless, because she is under the laws of her mother's birth country, she is still denied belonging in the country that, because of other ties, feels like home. Her father was Bahamian, and her grandparents, and their parents before that. That sense of rejection from the place called home is true in Case 1 as well. It is enough to make anyone feel like an outsider. When people's discretion and the laws that reflect them have more power in deciding where one belongs or does not belong, the church has to ask itself, what have we done?

Outsiders: That is what Hagar and Ishmael became. In my reading of this passage, they represent the many millions of people in this world who have been given this label because of their situation by those who have the power to dictate who they are and what they are entitled to.

Consistent with what was likely common practice in the passage's historical context, it is possible that, from the time of her birth, Hagar was simply a household commodity. Genesis 16:1-2 says, "Now Sarai, Abram's wife, bore him no children. She had an Egyptian slave-girl whose name was Hagar, and Sarai said to Abram, 'You see that the LORD has prevented me from bearing children; go in to my slave-girl; it may be that I shall obtain children by her.' And Abram listened to the voice of Sarai."

Bringing this text into the current global context, in this passage, Sarai and Abram could represent voices in the church that demand, enable, and encourage the handling of human beings as commodities today. In chapter 16, Sarai gave the order and Abram complied. In chapter 21, it says, "But Sarah saw the son of Hagar the Egyptian, whom she had borne to Abraham, playing with her son Isaac. So she said to Abraham, 'Cast out this slave woman with her son; for the son of this slave woman shall not inherit along with my son Isaac'" (9-10). Abraham became distressed, because naturally he would comply. But the voice of God intervened and gave Abraham some comfort in following the instructions of Sarah, whose apparent greed, insecurity, and fear were directing her conduct and guiding her sense of relationship with Hagar the Egyptian and her son Ishmael. After all, that was their way of life. It was likely how these household power dynamics normally played out as a result of the societal norms of their day.

In today's church, we also have at least those two voices: the voice of outright discrimination and the voice that is silent in the face of discrimination and turns a blind eye to it. Those who go along with it because it is the acceptable norm and then pray that somehow God will intervene, when human frailty means that the resources and courage to do so themselves is lacking. With Hagar and Ishmael, God did intervene, demonstrating that there is no one who does not belong, because all belong to God.

Outsider: That is what Christ became in order to intervene on our behalf. As the church, knowing what we know about the sacrificial, the bold, the extravagant, the messy, the liberating love of Christ, we therefore have no choice and we no longer have any excuse for continuing the same modus operandi that human beings have held onto in societies and households in generations past.

James Cone, known for establishing Black liberation theology, is quoted as saying that "Any theology that is indifferent to the theme of liberation theology is not Christian theology."[1] What this means is that we can no longer, in the Christian church, be satisfied with being the voice of Sarah or the voice of Abraham. Instead, we must be the voice and the face of God to the outsiders of our world. Since human beings have existed, in times of difficulty, confusion, war, and violence, the world's most vulnerable people are the ones who are commodified and become disposable, usable, discardable.

When Abram and Sarai were in distress and their life circumstances were not providing their needs as they desired, they used a woman with no status or voice of her own. Then, when Abraham and Sarah were blessed with having what they needed and wanted, they discarded the riffraff, and Hagar and Ishmael simply became baggage. Abraham and Sarah didn't see themselves as being responsible anymore for household commodities that they could no longer understand or control.

The church, as the household of faith, must now look honestly at ourselves. Many realities today make the church feel out of control. We have so

---

1. "James Cone," Bill Moyers Journal, PBS website, https://www.pbs.org/moyers/journal/11232007/profile.html.

many people in our societies today that the church doesn't seem to understand. Whereas, in the Caribbean region, our colonizers established a firm foundation of systems and doctrines of manipulation and control within the Christian church, the people in our communities are more often than not resisting anything that controls or manipulates. Women are embracing intersectional feminism, femininity is being seen more and more as a strength instead of a weakness, and we are understanding ourselves as created for more than being property or as helpmates to our partners, especially compared to traditional patriarchal gender role dynamics of heteronormative partnerships. Science, if we are humble enough to listen, has told to us that gender is a human construct, and in our region many children suffer to the point of being stateless, even with passports in their hands, simply because they do not conform to heteronormative ideals about gender and identity. Persons have been thrown out of their homes, families, and church fellowships in many instances. People of colour are loving ourselves and demanding that it be understood that our lives matter and that we are not commodities. That existing as a commodity will no longer be tolerated in many of the spaces it once was; now it is being met with more and more global uprising and resistance. Millennials and refugees are teaching us all that no walls can be built high enough to keep dreamers from reaching their final destination and places of hope, safety, and the promise of peace.

What, then, are we called to do and be as the face and the voice of God in light of progressive thought and perplexing realities, in a world where our women, children, and marginalized communities bear the brunt of the world's evils, as they are trafficked and enslaved in a 40-billion-dollar industry, as incest and church sexual abuse are as high as ever, as church-inflicted atrocities throughout history keep coming to light, and as sexual harassment survivors are finding their own voices, holding hands and screaming, "Me too!"?

How do we respond in our local communities where the outsiders are made outsiders by the only place they ever wanted to call home? Never mind that in the cases presented above, another country was willing to accept them. Is that enough? Should that be enough of a solution when the

Bahamas is the place your ancestors first understood as home after being ripped from home and parted with violence from the mother home? Can there be any solace in being denied a right to the same soil that your ancestors clung to beneath the shadow of the slave master and the almighty whip – and then after surviving it all by finding a place of peace somewhere between the African religions and the religion the colonizers brought, your ancestors built something: culture, religion, society? Journeying all this way through time and generations to still be told in so many ways that you do not belong. Rejected: an outsider by law. Why? Because, by law, so many of us are still considered property today. By law, your Bahamian mother, if she chooses to marry a foreigner, ideologically becomes the property of that foreigner, so you, too, must go. And if your Bahamian father was not, in theory, enough of a man that toxic masculinity demands he become to claim, as his property by marriage, the woman he impregnated, then you, too, must go?

When the church has perpetuated and encouraged gender discrimination by perpetuating the masculinization of God and all things God, when, in many contexts, the church has instructed our governments to remind women where their place is: standing behind, submissive to, and underneath their husbands, what have we done, church? What have we done?

Yet that is not as important as the question "What can we do?" That is what we are here to discuss and make come alive. We can commit to doing away with gender-exclusive language in worship, in prayer, and in the versions of scripture we cling to, which are no longer academically accepted as theologically accurate or helpful in interpreting with integrity of faith. We can, rather than skirting the issues, plainly and directly give messages professing total and unbiased equality for all people, regardless of sexual orientation and gender identity, being humble enough to acknowledge the church's perpetuating academically incorrect and bigotry-based interpretations of scripture for decades. We can speak out against gender-based violence and discrimination. We can agitate and advocate for legislative and constitutional change for women's rights – the ability to confer citizenship to spouses and children equally, just as men can confer their citizenship. We can put aside our insecurities in the face of people, ideals, practices, and realities that we don't as individuals understand and are unable to control in ways we've been taught are associated with God's church and reign in the world. We can vow to be more like God: when Hagar was sent away from the house of Abraham, God went with her and assured her that she and her child had a purpose; they had a place where they belonged. They belonged to God, as do Ricardo's child and Brittney and every at-risk or stateless person in the Bahamas, every human being on the face of this earth, and every created thing in this universe. There is no one who we as church can convince God to consider an outsider to God's reign. Let us remember this as we daily face the choice to be the face and the voice of fear, greed, and cowardice, or to be the face and the voice of a loving, compassionate, and generous God, who is almighty in strength and gentle in heart.

Amen.

Song
Xhoza and Zulu: "Senzeni Na"[2]

This anti-apartheid folk song is one of lament, asking, "What have we done (to deserve this)?" I invite you to reflect on these words as if you are hearing them from the lips of oppressed people who have become outcasts of the church and our societies. Please also consider the words as an internal lament, prompting us to be accountable in the presence of God for the ways that we willingly, including by turning a blind eye, participate in the oppression of others.

Prayer
Loving God,
it is not by mistake or by accident that we are here.
We give you praise and honour and glory for the privilege of your calling
and the assurance of your abiding presence
through all that we will encounter in this ministry and in your work.

---

2. "Senzeni Na (What Have We Done?)," https://www.youtube.com/watch?v=SJP79Zon3Ek.

Forgive us, God who sees and knows,
for we have often been cowards in our approach to your people in need.
We have often stood on the side of power and privilege when you have
    called us,
like Christ, to cast our crowns at your feet and surrender to your will.
Forgive us for our lack of compassion and our willingness to uphold
social constructs and ideals that cast some people aside and lift others up.
Help us to be more like you, God our Parent, who loved us before we
    were formed,
and who placed in us the seeds of your compassion and kindness and love.
Help us in understanding the radical love of Christ in our lives
to seek to do everything you would have us to do
to reveal that love to your people in need.
Help us to overcome the powers of evil in this world,
even when they exist in intimidating places, in governments and in the
    church —
even when they exist within us and our hatred and prejudices.
Bless us as we seek to liberate your people
as a sign of the presence of our liberating God,
and may your name be always and forever glorified. Amen.

LEST WE FORGET: A WCC WORKSHOP ON STATELESSNESS

KAREN GEORGIA A. THOMPSON

The Israelites Are Oppressed

Now a new king arose over Egypt, who did not know Joseph. He said to his people, "Look, the Israelite people are more numerous and more powerful than we. Come, let us deal shrewdly with them, or they will increase and, in the event of war, join our enemies and fight against us and escape from the land." Therefore they set taskmasters over them to oppress them with forced labor. They built supply cities, Pithom and Rameses, for Pharaoh. But the more they were oppressed, the more they multiplied and spread, so that the Egyptians came to dread the Israelites. The Egyptians became ruthless in imposing tasks on the Israelites, and made their lives bitter with hard service in mortar and brick and in every kind of field labour. They were ruthless in all the tasks that they imposed on them. (Ex. 1:8-14)

I want to begin my reflection with a poem I wrote. The title of the poem is "complicit." To be complicit is to help in some way to commit a wrong or a crime.

complicit[1]

measure the silence
in beats of compassion
how long before you speak
the world needs your voice
to speak while others weep
silence is for those who sleep.

measure the silence
in the breaths between their screams
how long before you hear
the sounds of hearts breaking
in defeat and despair
silence is for those who don't care.

measure the silence
in the depths of their teardrops
another child dies
in her mother's arms
hunger gnaws at their bellies
no food for miles
silence is for those spewing bile.

measure the silence
in the heart beats of the hopeless
cry because you must
because your soul aches for justice
grasping at peace
no need for despair
silence is for those who won't hear.

---

1. Copyright Karen Georgia A. Thompson.

measure the silence
in the syllables of repackaged truth
the system is abusive
justice is elusive
scream your truth
run from hate and fear
silence is for those who are living dead.

I was asked to provide a reflection on racial discrimination and belong-ingness. As I mused on where to go with this request, I received and read the first volume of *I Belong*, an initial collection of biblical reflections on state-lessness, edited by our sister Semegnish Asfaw.[2] Shirley DeWolf wrote the following in her reflection in that publication:

> As we move forward today with our plans for the church to challenge systems and structures that allow statelessness, let us begin with some self-examination to make sure we are ready for the task. How broad do you think our mandate is: Are we ready to take on the full scope of Jesus' inclusive ministry? Are we prepared to do the most we can rather than the least we can get by with, heeding Jesus' piercing question to his followers: "What more are you doing than others?"[3]

I believe these questions raised by DeWolf are relevant for us today and every day as we focus on Jesus' command that we love one another.

The issue of statelessness requires that the church critically examine its past, not in part but in totality, when it comes to racial discrimination in the Caribbean region and globally. The church in this context is not the church in Curaçao. It is not the church in Jamaica. It is not the church in the Dominican Republic. Nor is it the church in Haiti. Instead, I am speaking about the church, the body of Christ, at large. The church has unfortunately been at the heart of providing theologies of discrimination and oppression globally for

---

2. *I Belong: Biblical Reflections on Statelessness*, volume 1, ed. Semegnish Asfaw (Geneva: WCC Publications, 2017).

3. Ibid., 113.

centuries. These faulty theologies, which have fuelled oppression of peoples globally, must be interrogated and refuted. Racial discrimination and the resulting challenges present in the region are built on the history of enslavement and brutal treatment of Africans who were brought into the region and Indigenous Peoples who were inhabiting the islands when they were colonized.

Many in this region and globally would just as soon forget how 200 million African descendant people currently living in the Americas arrived in the area. The kidnapping, commodification, and exportation of Africans into the Americas – north to south, and in the Caribbean islands – continues to be a primary challenge in the region. The church was present in blessing slave ships and providing theological support for the enslavement of Africans. There were missionaries on those ships as well, taking passage into the colonies to bring a gospel to people considered to be less than human and maybe just a little more than animals. The plantocracy of colonialism required cheap labour: it put in place a system that has resulted in problems and challenges globally, while pushing Europe into the Industrial Revolution and beyond on the human and natural resources extracted and exported from colonized lands.

In 2011, I attended the assembly of the Caribbean and North American Area Council of the World Communion of Reformed Churches. The meeting was held in the city of Santo Domingo in the Dominican Republic. As with previous and subsequent assemblies, the representatives of the member churches were invited to participate in immersion experiences. We were there to learn about the myriad issues facing the communities in that context. We were divided into groups to meet with partners and visit communities around several pressing issues. As part of the group that visited the *bateyes* that day, I met with members of the Haitian community living in these areas where sugar cane is farmed.

We visited schools and learned about the work of the teachers in these communities, in places where children were denied an education. We learned about the ways individuals were providing care for and educating the children while their families worked in the fields. We met with teachers and heard their concerns for the children, some of whom did not attend school regularly. We met with medical professionals who were in the communities providing health care, and in some cases minimal health care, for communities that were stateless.

As we left the communities on the bus that day, I was staring out the window deep in thought. It is hard to see those experiences of people's lives and not be moved. We made our way slowly along the unpaved dirt road leading in and out of the community. Along the side of the road was a trench which carried the run-off water draining from the fields lining the road, fields in which many of the residents worked. The water was murky, a cloudy white colour that indicated it was not clean. As we drove by, I noticed the children swimming and playing in the water, undeterred by its filth. Further down the road, we passed an adult male with his back turned, washing himself in those same waters.

The issue of statelessness produces major violations of human rights and is a thief of human dignity and respect. Our intention is to address prevention and reduction of statelessness, even as we advocate for the human rights of stateless people and for laws that do not render people without home and country. However, we have to be willing to look at the ways in which we continue to contribute to statelessness and stateless people by omission and commission, because our silence, the absence of our voices, contributes to this escalating problem. Our silence makes us complicit. Our unwillingness to be advocates for change and on behalf of "the least of these" (Matt. 25:40) is contrary to the call to be followers of Jesus Christ.

I chose the Exodus passages to consider as we hear, learn, and discern the call to be active participants in advocating and intervening on behalf of the millions who find themselves without a place to call home. I want to focus my reflections theologically.

The story in the Exodus passage is familiar to most Christians. But I will make no assumptions and will broaden the content and context of the text. The story of the enslavement of these people begins in the previous book, Genesis. As the story goes, Joseph's brothers were jealous of the place he held in his father's life. He was the favourite child in their home. They plotted and schemed and sold him into slavery to get him out of the house, believing his absence would create a different set of dynamics between them and their father. They told their father that their brother died.

Years later, Joseph rose to power in the house of the Pharaoh. Joseph was instrumental in interpreting the Pharaoh's dreams and used his ingenuity to assist the Egyptians in preparing for a famine that ravaged the land. Because of that famine, Joseph's family ended up in Egypt after they came to buy food from the Egyptians. Joseph saved the day. When his family moved to Egypt, they were strangers in a foreign land, but Joseph was in a position of privilege and power in the house of the Pharaoh. But eventually Joseph died. His brothers died. All the people from that generation died. The Pharaoh also died, and with him went the institutional knowledge that protected the descendants of Jacob. Yes, people have a tendency to forget.

They forget about the people they brought in to build their railroads. They forget about the men and women who worked in their sugar cane fields and grew their crops. They have a tendency to forget that the people came and, in some cases, the people came because they were invited to do work that no one else wanted to do.

The new Pharaoh, the text said, did not know Joseph. He did not know how the Israelites came to be present in Egypt. He knew they were a minority in the community. He experienced their presence as a threat to the Egyptians because these Israelites were growing in large numbers. What would happen to the power of his people if the number of Egyptians continued to be out-paced by the Israelites? Seeing the Israelites as a threat, he devised a plan to oppress them in the communities in which they lived. They were assigned taskmasters who were brutal and who were more concerned about the build-ings being erected rather than the people who were being used as unpaid labour. They were given laborious tasks to do, made to work with account-abilities to the Pharaoh and the enslaved. Because of the Pharaoh's fear, he felt he needed to protect the rights of the Egyptians by enslaving the descendants of Jacob. As enslaved people, living in a country to which they had migrated, the Israelites had their rights taken away from them. They were no longer full participants in the nation.

The issue of statelessness is complex. *The Invisible Among Us* by Semeg-nish Asfaw documents in detail the challenges and plight of statelessness and accounts for the United Nations declarations related to statelessness.[4] The list of challenges facing stateless people includes, but is not limited to, poverty, homelessness, lack of health care, lack of access to education, and lack of access to jobs. They are denied basic human rights and fundamental freedoms. This is the work of systems that choose to forget. These are systems that perceive people as threats to power and as a result choose to further marginalize and discriminate against communities that are rendered stateless.

The WCC's Pilgrimage of Justice and Peace is a call for walking together in solidarity. The quest for peace must be accompanied by truth telling when we begin to address these global crises. According to the UNHCR report of November 2017, "More than 75% of the world's known stateless populations belong to minority groups."[5] Accompanying that number are institutionalized discrimination based on language, religious traditions, customs, and skin colour. Filippo Grandi, the United Nations High Commissioner for Refugees, said, "If we want to end statelessness, we must address this discrimination."[6] What has history taught us about discrimination and exclusion?

The biblical narratives in Genesis and Exodus date back thousands of years. Throughout history, we have continued to marginalize and persecute people because of differences. The history of African and African descendant people cannot be ignored in this conversation. Across Africa and what is now the African diaspora, the historic discrimination against African descendant people continues to be challenging for the existence and rights of African people. These historic forms of discrimination are present in legislative actions, discriminatory policies, the weaponizing of faith and gender, the marginalization of peoples, and the resulting experiences of statelessness, which is increasing. We must not forget.

---

4. Semegnish Asfaw, *The Invisible Among Us* (Geneva: WCC Publications, 2016).

5. UNHCR, *"This Is Our Home": Stateless Minorities and Their Search for Citizenship* (November 2017), 1, https://www.unhcr.org/ibelong/wp-content/uploads/UNHCR_EN2_2017IBELONG_Report_ePub.pdf.

6. Ibid.

The story of the Haitian people is mired in racial discrimination that dates back to the commodification of African descendant people and the trans-Atlantic slave trade. We talk about xenophobia, racism, sexism, and ageism, and to these we can add colourism or shadeism, which is not to be confused with racism. Racism is discrimination based on race. What happens when people are of the same race, but discrimination is based on the difference in skin tone or skin colour? That is colourism or shadeism. Who decided that skin tone or skin colour matters? Where did the preferential option for those of lighter skin come from? If we are to make advances in advocating for stateless people, we need to remove the barriers that are present as a result of all forms of discrimination, including racial discrimination and colourism.

Today, as in biblical times, there is a big problem in Egypt. Global oppression is growing, and we are here because we are being called to do something about it. We are the church. Are we willing to address our phobias and name our truths so that we might rise to the challenge of ensuring human rights and dignity for all?

I am often inspired by the story of the call of Moses, until I remember that he was not always the hero we make him out to be. At the time of the oppression of the Hebrew people, Moses was living in the house of the Pharaoh. He was a descendant of those whose rights were revoked; his mother had saved him from a similar plight by hiding him. He was found by the Pharaoh's daughter and raised as a prince. Moses knew who his people were. Moses knew that these people who were being oppressed were his people. And yet, we read nothing about Moses advocating on behalf of his people with his adoptive grandfather, the Pharaoh.

The Bible does not tell us how you could spot the difference between an Egyptian and an Israelite. Was it their customs that separated them? Perhaps it was the food they ate? Maybe they wore their hair differently. How different was their language when they moved to Egypt? Whatever the differences were, Moses was sufficiently assimilated that who he was in the house of the Pharaoh was not perceived as a threat.

Where are you on the issue of statelessness today? Could you make the case for some and not for all? Where are you in your examination of the issues that relate to statelessness, such as financial gains that are achieved? What does it mean to you that the men, women, and children who are stateless are not only without a place to call home but are being exploited?

Moses was called to be God's hands and feet in going to see the Pharaoh. We, too, are being called. We are being called to find our way to educating ourselves and addressing the many issues related to statelessness. We are being called to address the intersectionality of these issues and ensure that all have access to their full human rights.

Access to clean water, safe homes, dignity, and respect are part of the rights of every person.

> Then the Lord said, "I have observed the misery of my people who are in Egypt; I have heard their cry on account of their taskmasters. Indeed, I know their sufferings, and I have come down to deliver them from the Egyptians, and to bring them up out of that land to a good and broad land…. The cry of the Israelites has now come to me; I have also seen how the Egyptians oppress them. So come, I will send you to Pharaoh to bring my people, the Israelites, out of Egypt." (Ex. 3:7-10)

Come! The call is to prevention, reduction, and protection.
Come! There is an urgency that calls us.
Come! The time is now.
Come! There are women and children suffering in great numbers.
Come! God is sending you to bring God's people out of the oppression of statelessness. Our work is not only to listen or to write a statement.
Come! We are being called to be active participants in God's work in the world.
Come! God is sending us. We are being called out of our silence to be witnesses to God's love and to bring about the change we know is possible.

CHAPTER 6

STRANGERS IN THE LAND WHERE WE WERE BORN: BELONGING, STATELESSNESS, AND INDIGENOUS PEOPLES

JUAN CARLOS CHAVEZ QUISPE

Then the master said to the slave, "Go out into the roads and lanes, and compel them to come in, so that my house will be filled." (Luke 14:23; emphasis added)

Being born and living in the land of the ancestors is a privilege that not all Indigenous Peoples have around the globe. Genocide, displacement, and cultural assimilation are actions that colonialism imposed and continues to impose on Indigenous communities to break down their collective identities and disarticulate their connections with ancestral lands. In doing this, colonialism questions the individuals' place in society, forces them to live in the middle as not full members of society, and promotes individualism. Apart from undermining the Indigenous Peoples' sense of belonging, such actions contribute to keeping communities as marginalized, stateless groups in racialized societies. This reflection explores Luke 14:23 as a Bible quote that was used to validate colonialism in Latin America (*maya*) and caused numerous negative effects in Aymara communities throughout history (*paya*). Building upon these considerations, this reflection poses some positive actions to reinforce contemporary Indigenous identities as well as strengthen their sense of belonging and eliminate their life as stateless people in the land of their ancestors (*kimsa*).

Maya (one)

Luke 14:23 is one versicle at the end of the parable of the great banquet that was taken erroneously for a command during the 15th-century colonization of the new world and the Indigenous Peoples and native populations living there. The great banquet (Luke 14:15-24) is one of the parables Jesus made use of to explain his mission while sharing bread with the head of the pharisees and other guests during the Sabbath. This parable tells the story of a man who invited his friends to a banquet he was preparing, but none of them attended due to personal reasons. Then the man had his servants bring in the poor, the crippled, the blind, and the lame of the town; although these marginalized populations took part in the banquet, there was still room for more people to join. As a last resort to fill his house, the man told his servants to compel all the people on the roads and country lanes to come in. No data is provided to tell us whether the people from the country came into the banquet, but the wording in this versicle shows how dominant people behave when relating to others. The parable concludes with the man sentencing that none of his invitees shall partake in his banquet.

The story illustrates how power is used to set asymmetric social relations at the time the gospel was written. The master was a rich man who had a banquet prepared for his friends, made decisions about the events as they went on, and controlled everything using his will. The servants did what the master had them to do and reported their results immediately, without questioning. In mediating between the master and everybody else, the servants adjusted to the actions and implicit social relations hierarchically defined by the master. The invitees' decision not to attend the banquet shows their relation with the master as either fellow rich men or more powerful people. The marginalized in town likely left behind their daily activities to partake in the banquet. Not only does this action show eagerness to get into the master's house and enjoy a meal, but also it shows their decision capacity to join an event even though they were not seen as guests from the beginning. In contrast to such clear relations between distinct groups of people, we do not know how the people from the country might have reacted when compelled to come to the banquet. However, it is noticeable that they were compelled to come in and were not invited as guests.

"Compel" is a verb often used to ensure someone will do something or to bring about something by the use of force or pressure. Its use in Luke 14:23 suggests that people in the country were instrumental to do the master's will, not a group of people whose inclusion was welcomed beforehand. The master's selfishness is evident in both his indifference toward the composition of his guests – as long as his house was full – and his lack of interest about other people's will. Things were similar in the other actors' behaviour. The invitees made use of free will as equal individuals to the master. Despite their limitations in society, the marginalized in the town also made use of free will to partake in the banquet as guests. However, people from the country were compelled to come to the banquet. Although there are blanks in the story, the master used the word "compel" intentionally. The master employed this verb to ensure the use of force, pressure, or both to make his house full. Compelling others to do something they were not aware of or did not agree with is a problem Luke 14:23 poses: it reflects how asymmetrical power relations were established in the past as much as they continue to be a common practice in today's world.

Contrary to living according to the gospel's teachings, Luke 14:23 was used to justify colonialism as God's will and to force Indigenous Peoples to enter Christianity under asymmetrical conditions. Both the one-sided interaction process between the master and his servants and the differing treatment the master gives to other people indicate how the society Jesus talked about was structured. In addition, the sequence "inviting" his friends, "bringing in" the marginalized in town, and "compelling" the people from the country reflects how society was conceived by those in a position of power and privilege. The master attempted to impose his will on those he considered inferior. Since imposition is neither new nor restricted to personal will, it has also influenced relations between nations and groups of people all over the world in different time periods. To dig deeper into nuanced understandings of imposition in history, the next section illustrates how the Aymara communities adjusted to the changes colonial imposition brought about five centuries ago.

Paya (two)

Colonial imposition refers to the actions colonial powers do to subjugate people and control territories outside the metropolis and its core administrative area. As Indigenous Peoples living in the margins of dominant societies, Aymara communities went through numerous episodes of colonial imposition. The Aymaras live in the Bolivian and Peruvian Andean altiplano, which is a flat high-altitude region (3810–4200 m asl / 12 500–13 779 ft asl) bounded by even higher snow-capped mountains. Contemporary Aymara communities are heirs to a rich culture, speak the Aymara language, celebrate their own traditions, hold strong beliefs toward caring for Creation – which is locally named Pachamama or Mother Earth – and share a common history. These communities work together under the principles of solidarity, reciprocity, and complementarity and live in their forefathers' ancestral lands. Although land is the scenery where life occurs and identity gets reproduced, colonial powers treated land as a commodity. To expand on this process, I next describe two events of colonial imposition the Aymaras experienced in history and their impact on contemporary communities.

First, the Spaniards conquered the altiplano in the mid-16th century and built an administrative system upon pre-Columbian forms of organization due to its practicality and viability. While the Spanish language was introduced in the continent, Quechua was the lingua franca that most Indigenous Peoples spoke across the Andes along with their own local language. Aymara communities adjusted to such changes gradually by adopting new cultural elements as their own, and eventually new communities emerged in the lands of their ancestors. Ancestral lands were fragmented to create new administrative territories functional to the interests of the colonizers. Central altiplano Aymaras became trilingual due to their close interaction with Quechua and Spanish speakers who transited their lands on their way to work in the silver mines of Potosi. In comparison, Northern altiplano

Aymaras continued to live in their ancestral lands, remained mainly monolingual, and kept a strong identity.

Christianity was brought into the altiplano by the Spanish conquistadors. Instead of putting into practice love for the neighbour as the Bible teaches, the majority of Christians mistreated Indigenous Peoples, people with African descent, and enslaved populations due to racial prejudices, misunderstanding of the word of God, and greed. Indigenous Peoples learned the basics of Christian doctrine, despite the Spanish elite's opposition, and eventually syncretism created new images of God. Syncretism is a result of human interaction and an unplanned by-product of colonialism. Syncretism refers to the process by which non-Christian views of the divine adapted to Christian teachings and tradition and ended up attributing new meaningful characteristics to God. This is the case of popular Catholicism; it emerged in the altiplano after numerous Indigenous beliefs were incorporated as true attributes for Jesus, Mary, or patron saints to ease mass evangelization and make Christianity relevant for the altiplano population. Although the same process went on centuries earlier in the Greco-Roman world and set the basis of Christianity, Aymara syncretism gets criticized and called into question.

Second, nation-states emerged in the early 19th century after revolutionary movements fought against Spanish colonialism to control the lands and resources on their own. Abuse, violence, and exploitation against marginalized populations did not stop. Indigenous communities were excluded from the new political structures, and their lands were divided into smaller administrative units. Northern altiplano Aymara communities were separated by international borders between Peru and Bolivia. Unlike the territorial unity established under Spanish colonial imposition, the Republic of Bolivia passed laws and bills to disintegrate long-standing Indigenous communities, sell their land, establish private property as the only legal form for land tenure, and create haciendas. Some Indigenous communities engaged in trials to overcome such legal impositions and were granted the recognition of collective land tenure for their ancestral lands. These actions reinforce the idea that keeping the land is important to maintain the community's identity among the Aymaras.

The two colonial impositions described above are examples of the mechanisms used to make the powerless do what the powerful want. Imposition in racialized societies perpetuates power and privileges for some while putting the majorities in the margins against their will. According to Aymara history, religion was the first element colonialism took away from Indigenous communities and likely the first one to get merged to create new religious beliefs. Forced displacement caused cultural transformations and language replacement over time, and new organizational systems were imposed to control people and lands. Unlike prior views of the land as a relational locus with nature, the same lands where our ancestors lived and enjoyed life, colonial imposition transformed ancestral lands into delimited territories owned by individuals. Although freedom and self-determination were restricted and caused negative consequences on marginalized populations' identity, the notion of ownership of the land is the differential variable that affected Indigenous Peoples' sense of belonging and its subsequent life as stateless people living in their ancestral lands.

Kimsa (three)

Literal readings of Luke 14:23 were used to justify the colonizers' ruthless actions against Latin America's Indigenous Peoples during the conquest because of the idea that the master himself, who was seen as Jesus Christ, was the one who validated the use of force to compel the people in the country to come to the banquet. Instead of conveying an open invitation to join Christianity, colonial imposition brought about contradictory actions to have Latin American Indigenous Peoples believe and accept God as lord and savior. Christianity came in as Christendom and engaged in the conversion of large groups of people to turn them into servants due to their allegedly lower human condition. Not all was a lost cause, because God continued to work through faithful people's actions. Some clerics and pious people acted with compassion and shared the gospel with Indigenous Peoples and marginalized populations, so they get granted salvation by the grace of God. In spite of this, most Indigenous Peoples were objectified and suffered impositions because their humanity was and is still called into question.

Asymmetrical power relations is the element connecting the parable of the banquet and the methods used to bring the gospel into the new world. The gospel entered Latin America in the late 15th century and has had an impact on its inhabitants ever since. In the beginning, Indigenous Peoples were seen as soulless beings with little to no difference from wild beasts. Fear of the unknown and the lack of biblical references of people living beyond the sea led the conquistadors to engage in genocide and act ruthlessly against Indigenous Peoples. Timely interventions of priests and clerics committed to the gospel – such as Bartolome de las Casas – made it possible for Indigenous Peoples to be granted a soul and become human beings. However, the people in power did not recognize their humanity, and they continued to be seen as inferior human beings. Such a condition transcended time and continues to structure social relations in modern-day Bolivian society. We, the Indigenous Peoples, are seen as non-rational, defenceless human beings who depend on others to access knowledge and salvation.

Living in a racialized society where outdated ideas are taken as true produces negative effects on marginalized populations, especially when these ideas are internalized and transmitted from generation to generation unconsciously. That is, individuals who suffered, were mistreated, or faced negative experiences in life passed on such traumas to their children, who eventually saw their lives being determined by their forefathers' negative experiences without knowing the origins. Generational trauma caused multiple generations of Indigenous Peoples to not reach their potential; people in power took advantage of this and imposed their will following their biased perceptions of the world. How Indigenous communities dealt with it is a question I attempted to ask in this reflection through the history of Aymara communities, which is one of many histories that describe injustices perpetrated against Indigenous Peoples under colonial imposition. Imposition is, therefore, another aspect to consider when discussing how asymmetrical power relations limit the sense of belonging to undermined Indigenous communities and propel notions of statelessness.

Imposition against Indigenous Peoples has been naturalized in racialized societies to perpetuate the idea that physical differences correlate with social differences, and therefore it is strongly linked to discrimination. Discrimination is, unfortunately, more common than we may think and affects many segments of society, including Indigenous Peoples, people of African descent, undocumented migrants, orphans, the elderly, women, and other marginalized populations. Imposition and discrimination are two factors in systemic violence that was exerted over marginalized populations and eventually contributed to generational trauma in individuals and collectivities. As a result, the new generations carry the burden of their forefathers and are conditioned to remain in the margins without a full understanding of the social constraints that put them in a place determined by someone else's will.

Systemic violence weakens the will of marginalized populations and forces them to accommodate to social injustices that are often hidden in assumptions validated socially, yet still erroneous. The same is true for legal issues when referring to Indigenous Peoples and marginalized communities, especially when related to land and territory, as is the case with stateless people. In detaching Indigenous Peoples from their ancestral lands and forcing them to live there without their rights being recognized, the colonial powers passed laws and norms to structure society. As individuals with limited rights, the Aymaras live as stateless people who went through numerous events of imposition and discrimination. Although systemic violence is more psychological than physical today, Indigenous Peoples continue to fight for recognition as equal human beings in society. One element that Aymara communities use to overcome such difficulties is to keep together as communities living in the lands of their ancestors. More importantly, Aymaras' will to fight imposition by keeping their beliefs, culture, and language was more effective than acts of rebellion.

Historical accounts are full of references about the way the colonizers imposed their will over weakened populations; only a few of them paid attention to Indigenous Peoples' will. The same is true for other marginalized communities. Their will was not taken into account in the past, and little can be said about it. However, it is possible to hear what contemporary marginalized populations have to say about their perspectives in life and their needs. Instead of contributing to perpetuating colonial imposition with their silence, churches can and should work together with the marginalized to end injustice and systemic violence. The churches should listen to the word of God and see the world beyond their homes and local congregations placed in positions of privilege. The Bible contains numerous examples of God's love for humanity and care for creation and inspires us to live in communities where life is taken as a most precious gift to be preserved. The gospel's message of love and life in abundance is an open invitation to all who want to join a community of believers committed to accept differences and promote life with dignity to all human beings.

This reflection was an attempt to find connections between Luke 14:23 and the experience Aymara communities have with colonial impositions upon the verb "compel" as used in the parable of the great banquet. Aymara communities were compelled to enter Christianity by force and coercion. As a result, they were depersonalized and suffered impositions in different aspects of their lives, including their beliefs, spirituality, identity, and connections with the land. These communities were weakened and struggled to keep alive their values so they would not forget their identity, sense of belonging, and connections with their ancestral lands without the burden of living as stateless people. Although Aymara communities kept living in the lands of their ancestors, they don't feel like they belong in the land; they see their identity as changed, if not vanished. This life experience is similar to what stateless people live every day, and because of that a strong commitment to end such expressions of systemic violence is required from the churches and from fellow Christian believers.

Community-based models see physical, psychological, cultural, and spiritual differences as crucial factors to restore dignity and full humanity to Indigenous Peoples and, by extension, to all marginalized communities. These models advocate for structural change in society toward the recognition of difference as a positive element to enrich social relations and make relationships more meaningful. Such differences include wearing traditional clothing, not mastering the dominant language in the area, using Indigenous last names, or practicing non-Western traditions. From a broader perspective, and akin to other ethnogenic processes going on globally, Aymara communities are on their way to reconstructing their identities amid racialized societies to resist power and use this as a mechanism to overcome foreign control and imposition. In doing so, Aymara communities express their will to reject colonial impositions and fight for self-determination through the use of tools the colonizers imposed to keep their privileges and control the others in racialized societies. The Bible and its numerous messages of love for the neighbour and care for creation is the main tool we the believers can and should make use of to be faithful to our beliefs.

CHAPTER 7

IDENTITY AND BELONGING: REREADING OF THE GENEALOGY OF JESUS IN MATTHEW 1:1-17

LAWRENCE IWUAMADI

Introduction

The gospels of Matthew and Luke feature lists of Jesus' ancestors in the early part of their narratives. In Matthew, the genealogy is the opening pericope of the entire gospel. Readers are quick to overlook this lengthy list of names that become boring to read. Yet, it is impossible to overemphasize the importance and role of genealogies in biblical tradition. In the gospel of Matthew, it is easy to see that the genealogy serves the role of linking the two Testaments. It also establishes the Abrahamic and Davidic lineage of Jesus. The evangelist's interest in establishing the Davidic descent of Jesus to support his messiahship becomes a reason to reread the genealogy in the light of present-day debates around identity and belonging.

The theme of identity and belonging evokes other themes, including racial or gender discrimination, political nationalism, hospitality, and integration of migrants and refugees. However, our focus here is on those members of society described as "stateless people."

Who Is a Stateless Person?

A stateless person is someone with no nationality:

> Not being recognized as citizens by any state, stateless persons do not benefit from the protection of any state. . . . [Statelessness] is about being vulnerable, defenceless. Since they do not legally exist, stateless people are "invisible" to the state system, hidden, marginalized, forgotten, yet living in our midst. Invisible among us.[1]

There are an estimated 15 million stateless people all over the world.[2] These people are the most susceptible to human trafficking. They have no access to health care, no access to education, no right to vote. Stateless people cannot own property, open a bank account, or travel freely. They are born stateless or rendered stateless because of exclusivist national laws, gender discrimination, or lack of birth registration. They are stateless because they cannot validate their origins or lineage in a way that fulfils the requirements of any specific country.

We are therefore studying Matthew 1:1-17 with a focus on statelessness. The goal is to see how the understanding of identity and belonging in the text helps us rethink and re-evaluate efforts toward facilitating and integrating stateless persons into the society.

Understanding the Biblical Genre of Genealogy

Genealogies are lists of names put together to justify or prove the origins of a person or persons. This could then be the basis of claiming descendance, pedigree, rights, or inheritance.[3] It "is an orderly list of names purporting to record either the pedigrees of individuals or the assumed relationship of such

---

1. Semegnish Asfaw, *The Invisible among Us* (Geneva: WCC Publications, 2016), ix.

2. According to the overview and analysis of global statistics of the Institute on Statelessness and Inclusion in August 2020 (see https://files.institutesi.org/ISI_statistics_analysis_2020.pdf), the official count is about 4.2 million stateless people in 76 countries. Because only fewer than half of all countries in the world submit any data on stateless persons, the UNHCR estimates the actual number to be much higher. The overview concludes that "Since there have been no developments on such a scale to suggest that there has been a major shift in the aggregate numbers, ISI continues to use its estimate of at least 15 million stateless people globally."

3. See Moisés Silva, ed., *New International Dictionary of New Testament Theology and Exegesis,* vol. 1, 2nd ed., (Grand Rapids: Zondervan, 2014), 556.

groups as families, clans, tribes or nations."[4] An important characteristic of genealogies is adaptability or fluidity. It is possible to change the list by adding or erasing names or generations to suit the writer's purpose. This element could therefore explain the differences in the genealogies of Jesus recorded in Matthew and Luke.[5]

Genealogies may exist in an ascending or descending order.[6] Linear genealogies seek to create the link between an individual and an ancestor, or a group of ancestors, by listing the names of those who form the connecting chain.[7] The purpose of genealogies is to prove kinship relationships that regulate "social interaction, marriage, and inheritance, along with other social rights and obligations" or in linear genealogies, to establish the right to power or inheritance.[8] It is arguable that Matthew's aim is to prove Jesus' Davidic link to his audience.

Genealogy of Jesus, Son of David, Son of Abraham

We find in the first 17 verses of the gospel according to Matthew one of the two genealogies of Jesus in the New Testament. Placing it at the beginning of the gospel narrative, Matthew gave the genealogy an important programmatic role and made it key to understanding the entire gospel. Arranged in a chronologically descending order from Abraham to Jesus, it attests to the identity of Jesus and shows how he is the fulfilment of the promises God

---

4. R. A. Bowman, "Genealogy," in *The Interpreter's Dictionary of the Bible*, vol. II, ed. G. A. Buttrick (Nashville: Abingdon, 1985), 362.

5. Most Old Testament genealogies are in the books of Genesis, Exodus, and the postexilic period books of Chronicles and Ezra-Nehemiah. These were useful in establishing the roots of a person or of a group of people and as such were important for the social and political structure of the time (see Gen. 29:31–30:24; 35:22-26; 46:8-24; Num. 26:5-51; 1 Chron. 2:1-2. See also Gen. 46:11; Num. 26:57-62; Ex. 6:16-25; 1 Chron. 6:1-81; 9:10-34; Zeph. 1:1; Ezra 2:59-63; 10:9-44; Neh. 13:23-28).

6. Véronique Gillet-Didier, "Généalogies anciennes, généalogies nouvelles. Formes et fonctions," *Foi et vie* 100:4 (2001), 4.

7. Robert R. Wilson, "Genealogy, Genealogies," in David Noel Freedman, ed., *Anchor Bible Dictionary* (New York: Doubleday, 1992), 930.

8. Ibid. See also Bowman, "Genealogy," 363.

made to Abraham and to David. Jesus is from the root of David (Rev. 5:5; 22:16). He is the fulfilment of the promises God made to Israel and the accomplishment of the prophecies of the Old Testament.

1. The Text of Matthew 1:1-17

Matthew 1:1 is a summary verse that reads, "An account of the genealogy of Jesus the Messiah, the son of David, the son of Abraham." The evangelist then gives a list of names, starting with Abraham and concluding in verse 17, returning to the same three names in a reverse order: Abraham, David, and the Messiah.[9]

Matthew's style shows his emphasis on the Christological element embedded in the identity of Jesus, the Messiah, the son of David. Central to the messianic expectation of the Jews was that the Messiah must be of the root of David. It is therefore important that the genealogy show Jesus coming from the Davidic lineage through a sequence of historical progression, situating him within history. It links him to Abraham in a succession of former famous people, thus lending authority and legitimacy to his role and history.[10] He is the Christ, the son of David, an essential title of the messianic hope.[11] Jesus is the fulfilment of Jewish messianic hopes.[12]

2. The Generations

Matthew uses the expression "was the father of" (in some translations, "to beget") to reproduce the Hebrew meaning of history as the sequence of generations.[13] When he came to list Jesus (Matt. 1:16), he uses the passive voice

---

9. Gillet-Didier, "Généalogies anciennes, généalogies nouvelles," 9; see also Donald A. Hagner, *Matthew 1–13* (Nashville: Thomas Nelson, 1993) 5; Mervyn Eloff, "Exile, Restoration and Matthew's Genealogy of Jesus Ὁ ΧΡΙΣΤΟΣ," *Neotestamentica* 38 (2004), 77–79.

10. Gillet-Didier, "Généalogies anciennes, généalogies nouvelles," 9–10.

11. René Laurentin, *Les Évangiles de l'enfance du Christ* (Paris: Desclée, 1982), 314.

12. Raymond Brown, *The Birth of the Messiah: A Commentary of the Infant Narratives in the Gospels of Matthew and Luke* (New York: Doubleday, 1993), 67.

13. Yves Simoens, *Entrare nell'Alleanza. Un'introduzione al Nuovo Testamento* (Bologna: Dehoniane, 2003), 25.

of the same verb to express the unique way Jesus, being the Son of God, connects to human history. In that way, the evangelist highlights how in Jesus, there is an overturning of events in a manner that the history of humankind with God becomes the history of God with humankind,[14] thus picking up the theme of "Emmanuel," meaning "God is with us" (Matt. 1:23; 28:20).

Matthew divides the genealogy (1:1-17) into three parts: from Abraham to David (non-kings, founders of the dynasty), from David to the Babylonian exile (kings), and from the Babylonian exile to Jesus Christ (non-kings). According to the evangelist, each of these has a list of 14 generations. The first part, from Abraham to David, contains 14 names of 13 generations. The second, from David to the Babylonian exile, has 14 generations listed. However, we observe that in this section, the gospel writer suppressed or deleted four historical generations. Identity and belonging are essential to Jewish culture. This allows for intentional manipulation of names and generations when it is indispensable to achieving specific goals of a genealogy. It is possible for example, that the oracle of Jeremiah (see Jer. 22:30; 36:30-31), who predicted the extinction of the dynasty of Coniah motivated the author of the genealogy to suppress Jehoiakim.[15] In the third part, listing from the return from Babylonian exile to Jesus, there are only 12 generations. One would need to count Mary and Jesus to get to 14.

A frequent question about the genealogy of Jesus according to Matthew is the significance of the number 14. Some people suggest it is a simple multiplication of the symbolic number seven by two. Others think that Matthew's three times 14 is the same as six times seven, which points to six periods of seven generations that preceded Jesus. Jesus, as the last to be mentioned in the genealogy, will then open the seventh and final period. This explanation, though, does not account for the motive for arranging the genealogy in three groups of 14. A plausible reason might be the enthusiasm of the evangelist to show the Davidic descent of Jesus. The numeric value of the name "David" in Hebrew *gematria* is 14, which could have influenced Matthew's

---

14. Ibid., 26.

15. See ibid., 30–31.

choice of the number.[16] It may well also be that the evangelist was more interested in grouping the list of names into three, referring to the tripartite division of the Old Testament: the Law, the Prophets, and the Writings. Regarding the presentation of this genealogy, the only thing that one may say with certainty is that the goal is to establish the lineage of Jesus and his roots in the Davidic dynasty and in Abraham.

3. The Place and Role of Mary in the Genealogy

Hebrew genealogies rarely include or refer to women. Matthew, however, mentions five women on his list of Jesus' ancestors, and the place of Mary in the genealogy is unique. She plays a crucial role because she historically and biologically links Jesus to the preceding generations. For Matthew, Mary did not "beget" Jesus and has no dynasty.[17] He describes Mary's role in bringing forth Jesus in the passive voice: "… Mary, of whom Jesus was born, who is called the Messiah" (Matt. 1:16b). Jesus took on human flesh from Mary. She is the biological origin of his humanity. God is the father of Jesus Christ, though not in a human or biological sense. Jesus is eternally Son. God sent the eternal Son into the world, and the Word took flesh in Mary. Therefore, Matthew placed Mary between Jesus and Joseph, the legal father. She is indispensable to the manifestation of a mystery that surpasses the wisdom and order of this world.[18]

Our reflection on the role and place of Mary in the genealogy of Jesus draws attention to situations in many countries of the world where women are suppressed and marginalized. It reminds us of discriminatory legislation, customs, and traditions that do not allow for equal treatment between men and women. In at least 27 countries, a woman has no rights to transmit citizenship to her children. If a woman, Mary, was so crucial to the identity and belonging of Jesus, in a culture where women are hardly included in

---

16. Brown, *The Birth of the Messiah*, 80.

17. According to norms, the act of begetting can be ascribed only to a man. Another verb would usually be used to express the role of a woman.

18. See Simoens, *Entrare nell'Alleanza*, 28.

genealogies, there is reason for Christians and people of faith to challenge the injustices in those structures and countries that do not allow women to give their children the right to be and the right to be visible. No mother would want her child to be stateless and thus invisible.

4. Other Women in the Genealogy of Matthew

Along with Mary, we find the names of four other women in the genealogical list: Tamar, Rahab, Ruth, and the wife of Uriah (Bathsheba). Though the evangelist does not mention these women as part of the genealogy, but instead refers to them within specific historical contexts, the choice of these matriarchs points to the way Matthew intends to portray the unique Messiahship of Jesus.[19] What, then, do these women have in common in relation to the messianic mission of Jesus?[20]

Some argue that these were women of questionable reputations who benefited from the providence of God. To find them mentioned in the genealogy, therefore, points to the grace and sovereignty of God at work, despite human weakness. In the Hebrew Bible, each of these women had unusual marital situations, or as some would say, ties to sexual scandals. Nevertheless, each of them played an important role in contributing to achieving God's plan for God's people.[21] The scandal of Mary's supposedly illegitimate child (Matt. 1:18-19) would connect with these women.[22] Raymond Brown wrote, "It is the combination of the scandalous or irregular union and of divine intervention through the woman that explains best Matthew's choice in the genealogy."[23] It is, however, important to observe that neither the Jews nor

---

19. See J. C. Hutchison, "Women, Gentiles, and the Messianic Mission in Matthew's Genealogy," *Bibliotheca Sacra* 158 (2001), 152.

20. See Wim J. C. Weren, "The Five Women in Matthew's Genealogy," *Catholic Biblical Quarterly* 59:2 (1997), 288; John Nolland, "The Four (Five) Women and Other Annotations in Matthew's Genealogy," *New Testament Studies* 43:4 (1997), 527.

21. Hutchison, "Women, Gentiles, and the Messianic Mission in Matthew's Genealogy," 154.

22. Simoens, *Entrare nell'Alleanza*, 29.

23. Brown, *The Birth of the Messiah*, 74.

the early Christians looked at these women as sinners.[24] But if it were true that the genealogy of Jesus included purported sinners, then the contemporary parameters of identity and belonging that favour a certain class of people need to be challenged. Elitism and principles that favour a certain class of people at the expense of those on the margins should not guide these parameters. Unfortunately, we still live in a world that warmly welcomes the cultured and favours brain drain and the emigration of highly trained persons, with little or no consideration for the less privileged.

There are at least two other perspectives regarding the four women which are crucial for identity and belonging. One views the women as representing the gentile world. Tamar was probably a Canaanite (see Gen. 38:1-6); the same was true for Rahab (Josh. 2). Ruth was a Moabite, and because Uriah the husband of Bathsheba was a Hittite, we assume her to be a Hittite as well. Including gentiles in a genealogy that set out to establish the descent of Jesus affirms his universal mission.[25] It further challenges situations around the world where people experience exclusion, are denied citizenship, and are rendered stateless because of nationalistic and exclusivist legal systems.

The other perspective sees these women as people who played significant roles in the fulfillment of the promise God made to Abraham and to David. Through divine intervention, these women were crucial to saving the lineage at the points where it was closest to extinction.[26] Tamar played a key role in seeing the lineage of Judah continue. Rahab showed her faith in ensuring that God's people entered the promised land. By giving birth to Obed, the grandfather of David, Ruth guaranteed that this lineage continued (Ruth 4:13-22). Bathsheba became the mother of Solomon, ensuring

---

24. See E. D. Freed, "The Women in Matthew's Genealogy," *Journal for the Study of the New Testament* 29 (1987), 3–4, who wrote "the Jewish Christians to whom Matthew was writing no longer thought of those women as sinners but as heroines. There is evidence that in Judaism they had come to be regarded as distinguished women because each had done something beneficial to the Jewish people."

25. Hutchison, "Women, Gentiles, and the Messianic Mission in Matthew's Genealogy," 154.

26. Charles Thomas Davis, "The Fulfilment of Creation: A Study of Matthew's Genealogy," *Journal of the American Academy of Religion* 41 (1973), 520–35.

that he became heir to the throne according to the prophecy of Nathan (2 Sam. 7:8-16).

Together with Mary, these four women were central to God's intervention at crucial points in the history of Israel. In the genealogy, Matthew appears to suggest that though the history of the generations might be irregular, God made straight what was winding through the role of these women.[27]

Bringing this reflection home leads one to think of the hidden opportunities that the excluded, the stranger, the marginalized, the migrant, the refugee, and all those at the periphery of the society bring with them when they are welcomed, identified with, and accepted as belonging. The genealogy shows the providential plan of God in fulfilling the messianic promise by making use of people who are unacceptable to the status quo. In each case, the women mentioned in the genealogy showed extraordinary faith vis-à-vis the Jews of their time.[28] The genealogy therefore highlights the good that came from being an inclusive community and challenges our criteria of identity and belonging.

5. Conclusion

Biblical faith has led Christians to commit to the struggle for justice, unity, reconciliation, and peace in the world. Each time we read the sacred scriptures, we rediscover insights inviting us to genuine witness to the gospel message. The genealogy of Jesus in Matthew 1:1-17 shows that it was important to establish that Jesus fulfills the messianic expectation of Israel by placing him in the Davidic lineage.[29] It is about the identity and belongingness of Jesus: to a people, to a nation, and to a dynasty.

However, the universal character of the genealogy is unique and undeniable. It is unique that a genealogy that sets out with the goal of establishing the identity and belongingness of Jesus invites us to openness through the

---

27. Simoens, *Entrare nell'Alleanza*, 30.

28. Hutchison, "Women, Gentiles, and the Messianic Mission in Matthew's Genealogy," 160.

29. Eloff, "Exile, Restoration and Matthew's Genealogy of Jesus 'Ο ΧΡΙΣΤΟΣ," 73.

presence of women, gentiles, and people with apparently questionable life stories. It invites us to reassess our criteria for accepting others.

The genealogy concluding with Jesus opens a new epoch of eternal covenant. In him, the story of God and humans reached its goal.[30] The new covenant inaugurated in Jesus Christ challenges exclusion and opens the way to universal belongingness. Not only are the promises made to David fulfilled in the person of Jesus, but Jesus also embodies the accomplishment of God's assurance to bless all the nations of the world in Abraham. It is therefore remarkable that this genealogy ends up leading us to see that in Jesus Christ, no one is excluded, no one is left out. It challenges our understanding and interpretation of identity, belonging, and belongingness.

Statelessness remains a serious societal scandal that challenges our understanding of belongingness. The difficulties of stateless people are the difficulties of everyone. Otherwise, stateless persons will continue to be anonymous and invisible. Pope Francis insists, "The universal right to a nationality should be recognised and duly certified for all children at birth. The statelessness which migrants and refugees sometimes fall into can easily be avoided with the adoption of 'nationality legislation that is in conformity with the fundamental principles of international law.'"[31]

Christians and Christian communities can play significant roles in addressing statelessness. We can help in giving stateless people a voice and in making them visible. This is possible through raising awareness in society. Christians can draw the attention of governments to the challenges and risks faced by stateless people and the need to revisit laws that promote statelessness and discrimination. The genealogy of Jesus is thus an invitation to rethink our understanding of identity and belongingness.

---

30. See Brown, *The Birth of the Messiah*, 67.

31. Pope Francis, "Welcoming, Protecting, Promoting and Integrating Migrants and Refugees," Message of His Holiness Pope Francis for the 104th World Day of Migrants and Refugees 2018 (14 January 2018), https://www.vatican.va/content/francesco/en/messages/migration/documents/papa-francesco_20170815_world-migrants-day-2018.html.

CHAPTER 8

THE NOTION OF OTHERNESS AND THE MEANING OF THE STRANGER IN THE ORTHODOX TRADITION: SOME THOUGHTS ON SIRACH 44:8-9

STYLIANOS D. CHARALAMBIDIS

Some of them have left behind a name,
so that others declare their praise.
But of others there is no memory;
they have perished as though they had never existed;
they have become as though they had never been born,
they and their children after them. (Sir. 44:8-9)

Dear brothers and sisters in Christ,

The so-called sophiological literature, to which the Book of Sirach belongs, represented over time not only an inexhaustible source of spiritual supply but also a fertile challenge of existential speculation in the life of the church. It is not random, for example, that extensive excerpts from this literature have been used in the liturgical life of the Orthodox Church, in order to speak for the Christian tradition that I come from. These specific verses, though they haven't been used in Orthodox worship, express fundamental truths that can provoke a very fertile discussion.

The above excerpt of Sirach refers to people who left their indelible imprint in life and history and are mentioned through the passing of time from the next generations; it also refers to people who lived like they never existed, and their personal life course fell into oblivion. The people in the second category bring us close to the theme of this publication: statelessness. People who are stateless indeed live "as though they had never been born," and from that point of view they could be seen – in their vast majority – as the "strangers" of our rich biblical tradition.

In the Old Testament, we can find references about the criteria of attitude and behaviour toward a stranger. "When an alien resides with you in your land, you shall not oppress the alien. The alien who resides with you shall be to you as the citizen among you; you shall love the alien as yourself, for you were aliens in the land of Egypt" (Lev. 19:33-34; see also Deut. 10:19). The God of Israel "loves the strangers, providing them with food and clothing" (Deut. 10:18); he also defines one manner of law, both for his people and for the strangers (Deut. 1:16). The truth that "It is a miserable life to go from house to house" (Sir. 29:24) is the reason that the notion of hospitality is so heavily emphasized in the book of Job: "the stranger has not lodged in the street; I have opened my doors to the traveller" (Job 31:32). However, not irrelevant is the fact that the famous hospitality of Abraham is simultaneously the loving movement to the three passing strangers and the manifestation of the Holy Trinity. Abraham himself, the emblematic figure of what we call Abrahamic traditions or religions, motivated by his faith in God (Heb. 11:8), abandoned his homeland and his family environment (Gen. 12:1; Acts 7:3) and "he stayed for a time in the land he had been promised, as in a foreign land" (Heb. 11:9). During the last days, also, the assimilation of foreigners is so huge that, according to the prophet Ezekiel, God will allot them an inheritance in the land among the tribes of Israel (Ezek. 47:22).

Perhaps we haven't sufficiently realized the truth that even our God is the "stateless," "immigrant," and "stranger" par excellence. The second person of the Holy Trinity, the Son, comes lovingly from the self-sufficiency and security of the uncreated trinitarian communion, takes upon him the "form of a slave" (Phil. 2:7), and acquires from now on both the human adventure and the human tragedy. This divine "immigration" acts archetypically as a movement of solidarity and love toward the human being.

The birth of Christ took place under extremely difficult circumstances in a stable, "because there was no place for them in the inn" (Luke 2:7). Immediately after his coming into the world, the Christ was forced to follow the refugee way as he was prosecuted and threatened by a greedy political authority. "Joseph got up, took the child and his mother by night, and went to Egypt" (Matt. 2:14). His entire earthly life is a constant confirmation of the words of the evangelist John, who writes that Christ "came to what was his own, and his own people did not accept him" (John 1:11). His countrymen also didn't hesitate to reject him at Nazareth (Luke 4:29). In any case, he was fully aware of the fact that he was a stranger when he said that "the Son of Man has nowhere to lay his head" (Matt. 8:20).

With his notably expressive and highly dynamic teaching for the final judgement (Matt. 25:31-46), our Lord "lends" his name and his face to every human person who suffers and assures us that our attitude toward foreigners and poor people is a criterion that is of crucial importance for our salvation. At this point, our Christian tradition is more revolutionary compared to our ancient heritage. In Christianity, the foreigner is not simply under the protection of Xenios Zeus, as happened in ancient Greece, but God himself identifies with the stranger. This truth was clearly repeated by the Holy and Great Council of the Orthodox Church, which was convened in Crete in June 2016. In its text entitled "The Mission of the Orthodox Church in Today's World," we read: "The Orthodox Church's efforts to confront destitution and social injustice are an expression of her faith and the service to the Lord, Who identifies Himself with every person and especially with those in need."[1] Simultaneously, the parable of the Good Samaritan gives the Lord the opportunity to explain with purity and clarity not who is but who becomes the neighbour, especially to a stranger (Luke 10:30-37). Also, it is of great importance that our Lord chooses to express a great theological truth, namely, the spiritual worship of God, to the Samaritan woman (John 4:5-42): in other words, to a stranger.

---

1. "The Mission of the Orthodox Church in Today's World" (2016), F1, https://www .holycouncil.org/-/mission-orthodox-church-todays-world.

The notion of *ξενιτεία* (the state of being stranger) is diffuse in our biblical tradition. The man is a guest of God (cf Ps. 15:1), a sojourner and stranger on the earth (Heb. 11:13; 1 Pet. 2:11), gifted, however, with the ability to be "citizens with the saints and also members of the household of God" (Eph. 2:19). But this intense feeling of temporariness would be wrong if it is being explained as a glorification of the escape from history. In fact, it refers to an evaluation of history under the light of last days (eschaton).

Φιλοξενία (hospitality) is closely related to *φιλαδελφία* (brotherly love), and *φιλαδελφία* comes from the sense of the unity of humankind. "From one ancestor," God "made all nations to inhabit the whole earth" (Acts 17:26). The Christian ought not to neglect to show hospitality to strangers and is asked to offer it without discrimination and or complaining (1 Pet. 4:9). Into the kingdom of God, the Lord will reverse the roles and reveal all the dimensions of the mystery of hospitality, serving (Luke 12:37-38) and dining with (Rev. 3:20) the awakened servants who open the door to the master when he knocks on it during his second coming.

The notion of responsibility is closely related to our Christian identity. Passivity and apathy may function even as complicity. The Christian must not be limited to a cost-free piety – to a verbal declaration of support without substantial initiatives of solidarity. The role of our churches is prophetic. We are asked to be the voice of all those who, unable to say a word, stay speechless; the defence of all who are blamed; the shelter of all who are unfairly prosecuted; and the hope of all who are desperate (see Prov. 31:8-9). There are many examples of fathers of the church who raised a voice of protest: not only for unjust social structures but also for the inequalities of their era. Let their example be a reference point for all of us.

Today, phenomena like racism and xenophobia express egocentricity, pathological phobia, and necrosis of our spiritual sense. For the Church, the "other" is neither an enemy nor my hell, as part of modern philosophy claimed. In contrary, the "other" – even in the most tragic moment of his existence and especially in that time – remains a unique and unprecedented image of God. The Message of the Primates of the Orthodox Churches who were convened by the Ecumenical Patriarch Bartholomew in Constantinople on March 9, 2014, is clear:

> 4. . . . As a result of self-centeredness and abuse of power, many people undermine the sacredness of the human person, neglecting to see the face of God in the least of our brothers and sisters (cf. Matt. 25:40-45). Many remain indifferent to the poverty, suffering and violence that plague humanity.
>
> 5. The Church is called to articulate its prophetic word. We express our genuine concern about local and global trends that undermine and erode the principles of faith, the dignity of the human person. . . .[2]

In 2019, an inspiring social document, *For the Life of the World (Toward a Social Ethos of the Orthodox Church)*, was published with the approval of the Holy and Sacred Synod of the Ecumenical Patriarchate. It addresses contemporary social issues and articulates the social doctrine of the Orthodox Church. It focuses, among other things, on migrants and refugees:

> The twenty-first century dawned as a century of migrants and refugees fleeing violent crime, poverty, climate change, war, drought, economic collapse, and asking for safety, sustenance, and hope. The developed world everywhere knows the presence of refugees and asylum-seekers, many legally admitted but also many others without documentation. They confront the consciences of wealthier nations daily with their sheer vulnerability, indigence, and suffering. This is a global crisis, but also a personal appeal to our faith, to our deepest moral natures, to our most inabrogable responsibilities.
>
> The Orthodox Church regards the plight of these displaced peoples as nothing less than a divine call to love, justice, service, mercy, and inexhaustible generosity.[3]

---

2. Archdiocese of Canada, Orthodox Church in America, "Synaxis of Primates Concludes" (11 March 2014), https://www.goarch.org/news/releases/2014/-/asset_publisher/7NCu YdJYMvgG/content/synaxis-of-the-primates-of-the-orthodox-autocephalous-churches-concludes.

3. *For the Life of the World (Toward a Social Ethos of the Orthodox Church)*, §§ 66–67, https:// www.goarch.org/social-ethos.

I would like to end my reflection with an exquisite excerpt from the liturgical life of the Orthodox Church which is chanted during the Ὄρθρος (matins) of Holy Saturday. It has a special touching sense and poetically expresses the quintessence of our theology: here, Christ is characterized as the stranger par excellence. Let's dedicate it to all the strangers of this world:

Come and let us bless Joseph of everlasting memory, who came to Pilate by night and begged for the Life of all:

Give me this stranger, who has no place to lay His head.

Give me this stranger, whom His evil disciple delivered to death.

Give me this stranger, whom His Mother saw hanging on the Cross, and with a mother's sorrow she cried weeping: "Woe is me, my Child! Woe is me, Light of mine eyes and beloved fruit of my womb! For what Simeon foretold in the temple is come to pass today: a sword pierces my heart, but do Thou change my grief to gladness by Thy Resurrection. [4]

---

4. *The Lenten Triodion (translated from the original Greek by Mother Mary and Archimandrite Kallistos Ware)*, St. Tikhon's Seminary Press, Pennsylvania 2002, p. 654.

CHAPTER 9

A BIBLICAL REFLECTION ON THE TERM "FOREIGNER" TO OVERCOME STATELESSNESS

DR ELIZABETH JOY

This reflection attempts to respond to the question "Can we redeem the term 'foreigner' from being used as an oppressive tool in the reality and the fear of becoming stateless?" Pitching into the case of Assam and then a biblical reflection on the word "foreigner," it is concluded that our Christian responsibility to the issue of statelessness is to combat it by adhering to international law[1] and reaffirming our faith by taking a positive and practical meaning of the term "foreigner." This will enable us to love our neighbour as ourselves. Such an action will result in reaffirming their human dignity, identity, and security by safeguarding their national identity rather than flouting the laws and the faith affirmations in many contexts around the world by loving our neighbours as ourselves.

Exclusion and Oppression: The Pillars of Statelessness

In 2019, people in the state of Assam experienced a horrible attack. Back in 2014, Charlotte-Anne Malischewski wrote:

---

1. UNHCR, Convention Relating to the Status of Stateless Persons, 1954, https://www
.unhcr.org/ibelong/wp-content/uploads/1954-Convention-relating-to-the-Status-of-Stateless-
Persons_ENG.pdf.

The *Citizenship Act* allows for the deprivation of citizenship through deprivation, renunciation, or termination. While it is unclear how often these provisions have been used or how grave the resulting statelessness has been, it is clear that the language of the law grants the state power to produce statelessness.[2]

What happened in Assam in 2019 is seen only as a foretaste of what can happen to the rest of India. The situation can be summarized as follows:

As the protests against Citizenship Amendment Act (CAA) rages across the country, for Assam, the emotional roller coaster ride is a throw back by 72 years: a jubilation followed by an unwanted burden and trumped up fear of extinction.

If completion of the first phase of NRC had brought some exaltation in the state over identifying nearly two million "foreigners", CAA threatened to re-instate citizenship rights to a segment of them.[3]

Prateek Hajela, the state coordinator of the National Register of Citizens (NRC), reported that as of 31 August 2019, "a total of 3,11,21,004 persons found eligible for inclusion in the final version of the NRC. This leaves out a total of 19,06,657 people, including those who did not submit their claims. 'Those not satisfied with outcome can file appeal before Foreigners' Tribunals,'" Hajela said.[4]

The NRC is to date the biggest drive to verify citizenship in India. It is argued that this action of identifying illegal immigrants was taken up in the

---

2. Charlotte-Anne Malischewski, "Where the Exception Is the Norm: The Production of Statelessness in India," *International Human Rights Internship Working Paper Series* 2:8 (2014), 23, https://www.mcgill.ca/humanrights/files/humanrights/ihri_wps_v2n8-charlotte-anne_malischewski.pdf.

3. D.P. Bhattacharya, "CAA protests in Assam: Why it is different from the rest of the country," *The Economic Times,* 17 December 2019, https://economictimes.indiatimes.com/news/politics-and-nation/caa-protests-in-assam-why-it-is-different-from-the-rest-of-the-country/articleshow/72844673.cms.

4. "Assam final NRC list released: 19,06,657 people excluded, 3.11 crore make it to citizenship list," *India Today,* 31 August 2019, https://www.indiatoday.in/india/story/assam-final-nrc-list-out-over-19-lakh-people-excluded-1593769-2019-08-31.

state of Assam, targeting those who entered and settled there, primarily Muslims from Bangladesh after 25 March 1971, and deporting them to their native country.[5] It can be clearly seen that the NRC was mainly aimed at Muslims, and it is on the basis of religion that a large group of people was labelled as foreigners. Many loopholes prevent a person from getting the correct document to prove their NRC, especially people below the poverty line, as they are already deprived and denied justice in relation to their basic human rights, such as education. It will be extremely difficult for the marginalized sections to produce even a birth certificate:

> Children whose births have never been officially registered remain invisible, according to UNICEF. India is among the five countries—the others being Democratic Republic of the Congo, Ethiopia, Nigeria and Pakistan—that are home to half of the world's 166 million children whose births have not been registered, according to a 2019 UNICEF report.

In India, nearly 24 million children under five years of age did not have their births registered in the last five years, UNICEF estimated.[6]

Today, the term "foreigner," especially in the context of Assam, is a forced identity imposed on people at the margins which creates ambiguity and is a step closer to declaring them as stateless. Statelessness is thus an imposed identity that plunges people into insecurity with deprived, denied, and exploited identities. They are filled with fear and hopelessness. In such a context, when citizens are also classified as foreigners and deprived of their citizenship, what does "foreigner" mean to us today? This forces us to unpack the term from a biblical perspective and reflect on its impact to combat statelessness in India, particularly in the state of Assam, where it is increasing.

---

5. Ibid.

6. UNICEF, "Despite significant increase in birth registration, a quarter of the world's children remain 'invisible'" (11 December 2019), https://www.unicef.org/press-releases/despite-significant-increase-birth-registration-quarter-worlds-children-remain.

Biblical Reflection

Do not mistreat or oppress a foreigner, for you were foreigners in Egypt. Do not mistreat any widow or orphan. If you do, I the Lord will answer them when they cry out to me. (Exodus 22:21-23 Good News Bible, Today's English Version with Deuterocanonicals)

Unpacking the Term "Foreigner"

We find four terms in the Old Testament to differentiate people in a particular place: "native," "stranger," "immigrant," and "foreigner."[7]

John R. Spencer looks at the Hebrew term *gēr* (גר; plural *gērīm* [גרים]) and accepts "sojourner" as the frequent translation into English. He also observes:

The Hebrew term (*gēr*) is only one of several words with similar or related meanings. These include *nokhrī* (נכרי) usually translated as "stranger," sometimes as "foreigner"; *zār* (זר) usually translated as "foreigner," sometimes as "enemy"; and *'azraḥ* (אזרח) usually translated as "native."[8]

There exists a contrasting picture of the foreigner in Deuteronomy 7:1-2 and 10:18-19 as God's instruction to Israel.[9] The former talks about not sparing the many nations [foreigners], and the latter says that God loves the strangers [foreigners] and gives them food and clothes. It also later asks Israel to love strangers [foreigners]. The latter text (Deut. 10:18-19) points to a category other than a conquest. It forms part of the guidelines for Israel's ongoing life in the land.[10]

---

7. Jeff A. Benner, "Natives, Strangers, Immigrants and Foreigners," Ancient Hebrew Research Center website, https://www.ancient-hebrew.org/studies-interpretation/natives-strangers-immigrants-and-foreigners.htm.

8. John R. Spencer, "Sojourner," Oxford Bibliographies website, 28 June 2019, https://www.oxfordbibliographies.com/view/document/obo-9780195393361/obo-9780195393361-0266.xml.

9. William Ford, "The Foreigner," Belfast Bible College Newsfeed, undated and no longer accessible.

10. Ibid.

This Hebrew word that is translated as "foreigner" (New International Version) or "stranger" (NRSV) is primarily used for a non-Israelite living among the Israelites. This paper chooses to use this term *gēr* for "foreigner."

Gēr [גר] had no extended families; they were vulnerable and therefore classified among the widows and fatherless.[11] The earliest legal references to the treatment of the *gērim* [גרים] in the Old Testament are found in the Covenant Code and in the Deuteronomic Code.[12] They received a lot of practical help and support from Israel, such as the following: "allow them Sabbath rest (5:14), support them with tithes (14:28-29), include them in festivals (16:11, 14), allow gleaning (24:19-22), avoid taking advantage of them or showing injustice towards them (24:14, 17; 27:19)."[13]

After doing both synchronic and diachronic analyses of the early legal material pertaining to the Covenant Code and the Deuteronomic Code in relation to the term *gēr* [גר], Peter Jenei arrives at the following conclusions, which sheds light on our topic:

> 1) *The strategy of assimilation* was applied to smaller numbers of fleeing, converting, and intermarrying strangers. ... 2) *The strategy of maintaining peaceful neighbouring relations* was applied to special clans of strangers who possessed a unique lifestyle or profession. The case of the Kenites shows that the peaceful relationship was maintained on the basis of loose kindred relations. ... 3) *The strategy of subordination and oppression* was applied to larger numbers of mass-migrants. The case of the Gibeonites represents the phenomenon of mass-migration.... This oppression could take the forms of temporal corvée labour, perpetual slavery, or − in a worst-case scenario − even extermination. If these stranger inclusion strategies in Joshua-Judges are not mere literary devices but culturally adequate reflections of ancient Near Eastern and ancient Israelite social customs, then it could mean that the laws concerning the treatment of non-assimilated strangers and semi-assimilated sojourners arrived to a

---

11. Ibid.

12. Ibid.

13. Ibid.

context where a rather rigorous customary treatment toward strangers already existed.[14]

What we see in the state of Assam in India is citizens of a nation who are forcibly ripped of their citizenship and made *gēr* [גר]; even females are *gēr* right from the time of their birth, as their birth is not registered. The strategy of subordination and oppression is applied on masses of citizens or those who can qualify for citizenship on the basis of their religion. Here, the sly manner in which citizens are forced to go through the process of being stripped of the identity of a citizen and given the forced identity of a foreigner is explicit. India is thus producing stateless people as the norm rather than the exception. We are called to affirm that God loves all people: the term "foreigner" cannot be used as a tool to oppress, subordinate, and exclude people and make them stateless. People who have lived in, worked in, and contributed to the life of a state cannot be destroyed as stateless people. God calls us to affirm the positive, caring meaning of *gēr* [גר] so that we care genuinely, reaffirming their human identity, dignity, and security.

In many cases, foreigners who enter other countries due to conditions that don't allow them to lead a normal life – such as a famine, poverty, war, or their own government turning against them on the basis of their faith, or any such reason – become refugees in a foreign place. In fleeing their own lands and entering foreign lands, they are displaced, dispossessed, disoriented, disadvantaged, and destabilised. This is traumatic. The receiving countries, becoming the foreign or alien lands, have the responsibility of caring and sharing their possessions to enable these newcomers to live. Most of the time they may find mercy and grace in the countries they flee to and get at least their basic humanitarian needs met. When it comes to the stateless, however, their plight is deplorable. They become the least, the last, and the lost in relation to their self-identities and livelihoods, and they are

---

14. Peter Jenei, "Strategies of Stranger Inclusion in the Narrative Traditions of Joshua-Judges: The Cases of Rahab's Household, the Kenites and the Gibeonites," *Old Testament Essays* 32:1 (2019), http://www.scielo.org.za/scielo.php?script=sci_arttext&pid=S1010-99192019000 100007.

deprived of human dignity. It is here that we find that our faith needs to be translated into action to help them live. Many stories can be shared to say that when you give to the poor and needy, you give to God directly. To begin with, I can refer to Matthew 25:3-46. Let me reiterate something that stands out for me always:

> The mission mandate that Jesus proclaims at the beginning of his public ministry as found in Luke 4:16-20 taken from Isaiah 61:1-2, clearly spells out the reason for incarnation – God becoming a human... Matthew 25:31-46 emphasises the need for an ethical life where the poor and oppressed become inclusive.[15]

It is then that we live out our faith and our theologies become life-giving and living theologies. Christ's love continues to reveal God the father and continues to emphasize that the Spirit of God will lead us into all truth. So the Triune God should challenge us today and everyday to ensure that we live out the goodnews which Christ brought into this world making it visible in our own local contexts.[16] Empowering the poor and the needy becomes an important task in doing 'Living Theologies' that will enable us to redefine foreigners – especially the 'stateless' in this context, who are stripped off their identies as human beings. The process of empowering those who are roaming in search of basic human needs and its reward is seen in the following Tamil poem:

Padamaada koil bagavarku onru eeyil
Nadamaada koil nambarku angu aagaa
Nadamaada koil nambarku onru eeyil
Padamaada koil. bagavarku adhu aame[17]

---

15. Elizabeth Joy, "Living Theologies: From Whose Perspective " in *Living Theologies: Reflections from Diverse Specificities*, ed. I John Mohan Razu & Arun Kumar Wesley(India: Christian Institute for the Study of Religion and Society (CISRS) & Christian World Imprints, 2021), 6.

16. Ibid.

17. Thirumandhiram of Thirumoolar, Poem no. 1857, Project Madurai website, https://www .projectmadurai.org/pm_etexts/utf8/pmuni0010_01.html

The period of the above poem's author, Thirumoolar, is considered to be 6000 BCE, with the poems being compiled in the 2nd century CE. What matters here is not the exact date but rather the essence of what is believed – that human beings are considered mobile temples. A simple translation will be, "When people offer to God something (money) through a statue or a picture, it will not reach God. However, if something is given to the needy and poor who are the mobile temples, it reaches God directly." The emphasis here is that when one gives to the poor, one gives to God, just as Matthew 25:31-46 warns about the judgment day and the criterion on which people will be judged – whatever is done to the least of our brothers and sisters is done to God. The stateless people are definitely a group among the least, the last, and the lost. Our duty is to give them food, clothing, and health care and above all to meet them in their detention camps to get justice. God's mission calls for such action to address all forms of injustice. We can address injustice through our love for God and humanity, Matthew quotes Jesus:

> "'You shall love the Lord your God with all your heart, and with all your soul, and with all your mind.' This is the first and greatest commandment. And a second is like it: 'You shall love your neighbour as yourself.' On these two commandments hang all the law and the prophets." – *Matthew 22:37-40*

A brief peek into selected quotes from other faiths and beliefs broadens our horizon of understanding our neighbours of other faiths or no faith, calling humanity to love all people as we love ourselves.[18]

Christianity

> "Therefore, whatever you want men to do to you, do also to them, for this is the Law and the Prophets." – *Matthew 7:12*

---

18. "The Golden Rule is Universal," The Golden Rule Project website, https://www .goldenruleproject.org/formulations.

"And, behold, a certain lawyer stood up, and tempted him, saying, Master, what shall I do to inherit eternal life? He said unto him, What is written in the law? How readest thou? And he answering said, Thou shalt love the Lord thy God with all thy heart, and with all thy soul, and with all thy strength, and with all thy mind; and thy neighbour as thyself. And he said unto him, Thou hast answered right: do this, and thou shalt live."
– Luke 10:25-28

"Owe no man anything, but to love one another: for he that loveth another hath fulfilled the law. For this, Thou shalt not commit adultery, Thou shalt not kill, Thou shalt not steal, Thou shalt not bear false witness, Thou shalt not covet; and if there be any other commandment, it is briefly comprehended in this saying, namely, Thou shalt love thy neighbour as thyself. Love worketh no ill to his neighbour: therefore love is the fulfilling of the law" *– Romans 13:8-10*

"For all the law is fulfilled in one word, even in this; Thou shalt love thy neighbour as thyself." *– Galatians 5:14*

"What you hate, do not do to anyone." *– Deuterocanonical Bible, NRSV, Tobit 4:15, Roman Catholic Church and Orthodox Christianity*

Confucianism

"One word which sums up the basis for all good conduct…loving kindness. Do not do unto others what you would not want done to yourself."
– Analects of Confucius 15.23

Greek Philosophers

"We should behave to friends as we would wish friends to behave to us."
– Aristotle

"Do not do to others what would anger you if done to you by others."
– Socrates

"What you would avoid suffering yourself, seek not to impose upon others." – *Epictetus*

Hinduism

"One should not behave towards others in a way which is disagreeable to oneself. This is the essence of morality. All other activities are due to selfish desire." – *Mahabharata, Anusasana Parva 113.8*

Humanism

"Don't do things you wouldn't want to have done to you." – *British Humanist Society*

Islam

"Not one of you truly believes until you wish for others that which you wish for yourself." – *The Prophet Mohammed Hadith*

"Additionally, the Prophet Muhammad said there is no excuse for committing unjust acts: 'Do not be people without minds of your own, saying that if others treat you well you will treat them well, and that if they do wrong you will do wrong to them. Instead, accustom yourselves to do good if people do good and not to do wrong (even) if they do evil.'" – *Al-Tirmidhi*

Jainism

"In happiness and suffering, in joy and grief, we should regard all creatures as we regard our own self." – *Lord Mahavir 24th Tirthankara*

Judaism

"What is hateful to you do not do to your neighbour. This is the whole Torah [Law]; all the rest is commentary." – *Hillel Talmud, Shabbat 31a*

Utilitarianism

"To do as one would be done by, and to love one's neighbour as oneself, constitute the ideal perfection of utilitarian morality." – *John Stuart Mill*

Unitarian Universalism

"We affirm and promote respect for the interdependent web of all existence of which we are a part." – *Unitarian Universalism Principles*

Across the board, all faiths and beliefs emphasize that we treat our neighbour as ourselves. In the case of Assam, people who have lived and worked as neighbours are made foreigners and made the stateless. I prefer to refer to the prevailing injustice to the stateless by the acronym SEIGE (Statelessness, Economic disparity, Identity crises, Gender inequality, and Enslavement). The role model and the solution for us as Christians is indeed Christ. In "Byzantine Concepts of the Foreigner", Helene Ahrweiler shows that these groups were considered as quintessential "others"[19]. She also indicates Christianization as a 'pivotal element' in the process that led to bridging the gap between the perceived sharp cultural difference.[20] Today the 2022 WCC assembly theme, "Christ's love moves the world to reconciliation and unity," opens our eyes and hearts beckoning us to welcome people of all faiths and no faith especially the foreigners who are seen as refugees or 'nobody'. This is one of the ways to realize the assembly theme in our world to bring about a transformation, especially in the context of the above realities. It is not just in Christianity or Saivism (deemed to be part of Hinduism, even though Saivites refuse this inclusion) that we find such a call for serving others with love.

---

19. Helene Ahrweiler, "Byzantine Concepts of the Foreigner: The Case of the Nomads" in Studies on the Internal Diaspora of the Byzantine Empire, eds Hélène Ahrweiler and Angeliki E. Laiou. (Harvard: Harvard University Press,1998), 5.

20. Mariusz Pandura, "Perceiving Otherness, Creating Resemblance - the Byzantinization of Nomads in the Age of Justinian I: The Arabs," *Acta Euroasiatica 1*, (2013) , 44. https://www .researchgate.net/publication/268519574_Perceiving_otherness_creating_resemblance_-_ the_Byzantinization_of_nomads_in_the_age_of_Justinian_I_the_Arabs.

God's love that sent God's only Son into this world, supporting and strengthening us through the Holy Spirit, empowers us to love our neighbours truly. This will pave the way to revisit the identity of 'Stateless' imposed on foreigners with specific reference to Assam in India.

Conclusion

In India, where class, caste, race, gender, and socio-economic and religio-cultural identities play a vital role, Assam is a troubling example. If we need to save the citizens of India, especially the Muslims and people at the periphery, from the clear strategies of the minority elite Brahmanical rule of the Indian government, we will have to question the idea, identity, and understanding of a "foreigner." In Assam, citizens are being treated much worse than the way "foreigner" was understood in terms of *gēr* [גר]. Our Christian calling is to stand by these minority religious groups and others who are being preyed upon and to boldly say that on the basis of our faith, we stand by the international law that does not permit a person to be made stateless, making them *gēr* [גר] foreigners. Thus, Christ's love urges us to have a positive understanding of the contrasting term "foreigner,". We can redeem this term from being used as an oppressive tool in the reality and the fear of making people stateless. We are called to love our neighbours as ourselves and not to dehumanize people by naming them foreigners and then imposing the identity of stateless on them. In the postmodern era, where we talk about a global village, we must look upon "foreigners" as our neighbours. Doing to others what we would like others to do for us is indeed the key to understanding the term foreigner in order to overcome the imposed identity – 'stateless' on the so-called foreigners in the State of Assam in India and anywhere else where people suffer such an identity crisis.